BLOOD MYSTERIES

When Innocent Blood Cries

Dr. Victor T. Nyarko

authorHOUSE®

AuthorHouse™
1663 Liberty Drive
Bloomington, IN 47403
www.authorhouse.com
Phone: 833-262-8899

Published by AuthorHouse 04/16/2024

ISBN: 979-8-8230-2184-5 (sc)
ISBN: 979-8-8230-2183-8 (e)

Library of Congress Control Number: 2024902914

Print information available on the last page.

PRESENTED TO

FROM

____

DATE

____

Other Exciting Books by the Author.

DIVINE EMPOWERMENT

This book is an exposition on the power of the efficacious blood of Jesus Christ, the legacy and empowerment it provided for the first Apostles, for today's believer in Jesus Christ and for all who will come after. It reveals the resources that God through Christ has made available and at our disposal for the successful accomplishment of the great commission. It also teaches the reader, how one can tap into these resources by believing it, claiming it, and possessing it.

ISBN9-78148

A DISCONNECTED GENERATION

This book presents striking differences between the génération of Moses and the génération of Joshua. Although Joshua's génération witnessed a glimpse of the miracles and wonder workings of God, they lacked a personal relationship with the God of their fathers and the God of Israel.

ISBN 1-59330-075-1

DEALING WITH REJECTION

Rejection of o n e k i n d or another is inevitable throughout ones' life; therefore, any tool that can be acquired to help deal with it should be a welcome choice. In this book, Dr. Nyarko presents the key elements that lead to the feeling of rejection and how to deal with rejection from a biblical perspective.

ISBN1-59330-471-4

BEAUTY FOR ASHES

It has been the church's traditionn to think that

great revival could be sparked by extensive advertising, putting up the right preacher and playing the right music. If these are true ingredients for revival, then John the Baptist' revival which ignited and blazed a trail in the desolate and obscure wilderness of Judea wouldn't have had the impact it did. On the contrary, out of the ashes of repentance comes revival, refreshing rrestitution and restoration.

ISBN 1-59330-605-9

WHERE ARE THE FATHERS

The lack of fathers at home has been one of society's greatest dilemmas of our time. This book has a timely word from the Lord for everyone. God our father is calling all fathers through the pen of this godly author and father, back to the honorable and critical role of fatherhood. Get ready, read it, repent, and pass it on. **ISBN13:9781593302436**

KINGDOM WORSHIP

Music is part of worship, but good music alone does not constitute worship. In this book, the various Hebrew words for 'praise' are described. It sheds light on the true meaning of worship and what the popular command 'Hallelujah' means in the praise and worship of God. It comes from the two Hebrew words *Halal* which is the most radical form of praise and *Yah* which is the short form for Jehovah. To worship God, goes far beyond being an act. It should be a personal encounter with God's presence which should lead to the worshipper, leaving His presence with fulfillment and gratification. In brief, this book focuses on what it means to halal (praise) God, who ought to Halal (praise) Him and where he ought to be Halal (praised). **ISBN 978-1-4984-3509-3**

THE PRODIGAL FATHER

What has become popularly but also erroneously referred to as the story of the 'prodigal son' is part of a larger revelation that Jesus wanted to show his church. This book then culminates with the distinction that our Lord Jesus makes between Sonship and servanthood in his vineyard parable about the servants and sons who were sent out by the Lord to work on his vineyard. Are all humanity Sons of God through procreation as many claims? Or is there a distinction between Kingdom-Sons and Kingdom-Servants of God? This book's approach to the story will leave you amused, instructed, enlightened, stirred up, and challenged, but not bored! **ISBN: 978-1-947349-23-0**

THE ORDER OF MELCHIZEDEK

This book takes the reader on an intriguing and interesting journey into the life and person, of a strange and isolated but unique bible personage called Melchizedek, He appears momentarily on the scene of bible history with the great Patriarch Abraham and then disappears from the pages of history just as suddenly as he appeared. All other references in the bible about him is traced back to this one occasion. He is said to be without father, mother, nor descent, having neither beginning of days, nor end of life. So, the questions then is who was Melchizedek? In what ways does his priestly order align

with the Lord Jesus and yet differs from the Aaronic order of Priesthood? Why should Melchizedek, and he alone, of all the Old Testament characters be thought of in a way that defies human mortality? This book's approach to the life and person of Melchizedek will leave you amused, instructed, enlightened, stirred up, and challenged, but not bored!
ISBN: 978-1-947349-21-6

THE 4 DEGREES OF RELATIONSHIP

It's a matter of common knowledge that many of the headaches one goes through in life are because of bad associations. This book is about relationships, friendships, and associations, which is one of the key areas of our lives that we need to safeguard against. The key goal of this book is to teach the reader how to model their sphere of relationship after the pattern of Christ. We all, to some degree, have a sphere of association with other people who have the potential to impact the way we behave and the decisions we make in life. As the say goes, "no man is an Island," because we are all interconnected in one way or the other. That is why as humans, and by instinct people will put their lives in danger to save even strangers whom they do not know or have ever met.

One cannot underestimate the importance that Jesus placed on his associations because it is out of his associations that he chose the 12 disciples who he would later refer to as his friends. It was also out of the 12 disciples that he later chose the 3 disciples (Peter, James, and John) who became his inner circle and confidants. **ISBN: 9781642371093 eISBN: 9781642371086**

ANTIDOTE: HOW THE BLOOD OF THE LAMB GOES TO WORK FOR THE SINS OF HUMANITY

The subject of the blood of the Lamb is one of the most common topics of discussions, teachings, and sermons in the Christian circles. It was L.D. Bevan that said, "The subject of the blood of the Lamb of God and the mystery surrounding this subject, will ever remain one of the richest gold mines of evangelical thought. It occupies a central position in the doctrine of atonement, just like the phrase "God is Spirit" in John 4;24, occupies in relation to the doctrine of God." There is literally no Sunday that one would leave an Apostolic or Pentecostal church service without hearing the mention of the blood in one way or the other. Even casual, everyday conversations among born-again Believers, often triggers the usage or reference to the blood of Jesus. Many know about the fact that there is power in the blood of Jesus. Many are also very much aware of the redemptive power in the blood of the Lamb of God and how to plead that blood against the works of the enemy in a spiritual warfare. However, a good percentage of Believers in our churches today have very little or no knowledge about why the blood of Jesus is referred to as the Blood of the Lamb of God and the dynamics behind how the Blood of the Lamb goes to work on the behalf of humanity against sin or the devices of the devil. The purpose of this book is to unveil the revelation behind the central role the Blood of Jesus plays in our redemption and how its power goes into play against the sins of humankind.

ISBN: 9781642371093
eISBN: 9781642371086

BLOOD AND FIRE

This book is about the biblical story of Cain and Abel, the first products of human procreation through Adam and Eve. This story is unique in that there are a couple of things done that were unknowns to human history. It is a story that although began with God's judgement against sinful human nature inherited through Adam and Eve, however, it ends with the powerful act of redemption that only comes from a God of second chances. This book is about the biblical story of Cain and Abel, the first products of human procreation through Adam and Eve. This story is unique in that there are a couple of things done that were unknowns to human history. It is a story that although began with God's judgement against sinful human nature inherited through Adam and Eve, however, it ends with the powerful act of redemption that only comes from a God of second chances.

ISBN: 1665507268

FORMER AND LATTER RAINS

God said, ***"I will pour out My Spirit in the last days upon all flesh".*** This began at Pentecost only as minor beginning. Before Christ's return, the Holy Spirit will precede in immanence, power, and glory, to prepare the church, because Christ isn't coming for a defeated church still struggling with sin and divisions, but a glorious church without spot nor wrinkle. The dimension of outpouring of God's Spirit will depend on how desirous the church is for His presence. After the earth opens its mouth due to dryness and desire rain from God, former and latter rains of revival are the fulfillment of this desire. Isaiah 37:3b ***says for the children are come to birth and there is not strength to deliver.*** May it never be said of today's church that we came close to birth and had no strength to deliver. ***Read, Repent, Be Revived.***

ISBN: 9798823004107

DEDICATION

This book is dedicated to my wife Joan Elaine,
my life-long companion, and best friend,

To

Our three precious children Victoria, Vanya and Joash who have dedicated their lives to serving God and been an integral part of the work the Lord has called us to do. Above all, their lives has been godly example of the gospel of Jesus Christ to their generation.

Their lives are the delight of any godly parent.

CONTENTS

ACKNOWLEDGEMENT

Many thanks to the following people for your selfless service in making this book a possibility.

Editorial:
Author House Publishing Editorial Team

Photography:
Victoria Nyarko
(VFWC, Bronx, New York)

Cover Design:
Author House Publishers

INTRODUCTION

One thing that every religion has in common, whether it is godly or ungodly, Christianity or occultism, satanic or otherwise, is the fact that they all respects blood and has something in one way or the other to do with blood. They all have either ritual practices that are based on blood sacrifices or doctrinal beliefs that are embedded in blood or are blood based. I always say that both the Jewish Torah and the Christian bible are bloody books. This is because blood is central to both the Old and New Testament beliefs and practices. After Adam and Eve sinned in the garden of Eden, the story of man's redemption has been that of a journey that began with the shedding of blood in the garden of Eden and ended with the shedding of blood at Calvary. In-between Eden and Calvary were the numerous sacrifices and religious practices involving the blood of bulls and goats in the Old Testament, with which the sins of the nation of Israel was covered by year after year until the final price of atonement was paid through the crucifixion of Christ for the entire human race.

As I investigated the subject of blood in both the Old and New Testaments over the years, I found out that there are great mysteries surrounding blood in general and the blood of Jesus Christ in particular that humans may not fully understand until the day when God through His son Jesus Christ would grant us grace to enter the pearly gates of heaven.

For now, we are as men who sees only dimly as through a mirror or glass according to I Corinthians 13:12.

[12] For now we see through a glass, darkly; but then face to face: now I know in part; but then shall I know even as also I am known.

But when Christ shall be revealed, then shall the fullness of the mysteries in blood be revealed also onto us. Then shall we have a full understanding of what blood is, and its role in God's vast creation. Until then, we may have many unanswered questions to ponder about. Just to list a few of these questions, have you ever wondered about what makes blood a unique fluid in the body of living creatures besides all other fluids. Or why blood takes on a red color in humans and other mammals, yet its blue in the octopus and other cretaceous animals and green in skink lizards and other creatures of its kind.

For now, we know just enough to know that the life of any flesh lives in its blood. Hence blood is the container of life, according to Leviticus 17. Since life is precious, perhaps that's what makes blood, which is the container of life, also precious. It is worth noting that the existence of blood did not begin with its existence in earthly creatures, including mankind. The bible makes us to understand clearly that blood existed long before it was ever made present in earthly creatures of any kind. In whatever form, state, or container it existed in, is beyond the knowledge and comprehension of humankind. The bible however makes us to understand that *"the Lamb of God was slain before the foundations of the world".* "Before the foundations of the world" obviously refers to a season or time before the worlds were framed into being by God and before all creation was brought forth from the womb of God. What this means is that the existence of blood predates its presence in all physical living creatures including mankind.

If you grew up in church, I believe you may have been taught at some point in time either through attending children's Sunday school or via a bible studies or sermon about blood of how that the blood of Jesus is powerful. I believe you also got to learn one or more church songs at least that evolves around the power in the blood of Jesus. In fact, in the Pentecostal-Apostolic church circles one would agree with me that there are more songs about the power of the blood of Jesus than any other subject matter that's spiritual. However, what the church has not investigated much into, is the revelation of what makes blood to command so much power. Therefore, although most of our songs had to do with power in blood, the church of today has not yet fully come to grasp of the understanding of what makes blood in general powerful and the blood of Jesus Christ even more powerful and capable to redeem humankind once and for all.

This book is therefore an attempt to explore some of the mysteries in blood. I used the word 'some' because for now the bible says we know in part, and we understand in part until that which is perfect shall be revealed. Hence with this partial knowledge in mind coupled with deep revelatory insights from the Holy Spirit, please join me on this intriguing journey of investigation through the pages of this book to explore the known mysteries of blood in general and the blood of Jesus in particular.

CHAPTER ONE

DIVINE SYSTEM OF JUSTICE

One ought to understand that the realm of the spirit operates according to eternally established spiritual laws, because no kingdom, visible or invisible, can be governed without laws. These laws forms what is known as God's divine system of justice. Just like every nation on earth has its own justice system so is heaven. These laws operate in the universal courts of heaven. To fully understand the subject of blood in general, and the power of the blood of Jesus in particular, we will need to critically examine some of the components of this divine system of justice. The first of these laws of God's divine system of justice that needs to be established can be found in Ezekiel 18:4. It states,

> *Behold, all souls are mine; as the soul of the father, so also the soul of the son is mine: the soul that sinneth, it shall die. (Ezekiel 18:4)*

The laws of God's divine system of justice are discrete and irrefutable laws of the spirit, and hence they are nonnegotiable.

Through the above scripture, what God is saying to humanity is that regardless of one's color, race, ethnicity, gender, or nationality, all souls rightfully belong to Him. This is a fact that one cannot argue about simply because we did not create ourselves. If we are creatures, then it implies there is a creator. The pivotal point established through this scripture is what God says about the soul: *"The soul that sinneth, it shall die."*

The second law of God's divine system of justice that I want to emphasize can be found in Hebrews 9:22. It states,

---

And almost all things are by the law purged with blood; and without shedding of blood is no remission.

Looking at the two laws of God's divine system of justice above, the first states that the reward for sin is spiritual death, and the second states that the remedy for spiritual death, should a person sin, is the shedding of blood.

What the above statement means is that, should a person sin, one cannot negotiate oneself out of the predetermined consequences for sin because these laws are predetermined by God and unchangeable. What this means is that no creature, terrestrial or celestial, including God Himself, who made these laws, could circumvent these laws should they be broken. In other words, should these laws be broken, the only way to get around them is to provide the prescribed remedy for sin, which according to Hebrews 9:22, has to do with the shedding of blood and nothing else besides that.

Another point I would like to emphasize is that the shedding of the blood of Jesus had more to do with the demands of God's divine system of justice than it had to do with mercy. Often, we tend to put mercy before divine justice, but that's just like putting the cart before the horse. This is because mercy came into the picture only after divine justice had demanded that the ultimate price for humankind's redemption ought to be met through the shedding of blood, according to Hebrews 9:22: *"Without the shedding of blood, there is no remission of sins."*

The shedding of the blood of Jesus had more to do with divine justice than it had to do with mercy. Mercy came into the picture only after divine justice had demanded an ultimate price for redemption through the shedding of blood.

Therefore, even if Christ Jesus were to die without the shedding of His blood, His death alone could not be enough to satisfy the demands and requirement for atonement of sin.

We often sing songs like "There is power in the blood of Jesus." Yes indeed there is tremendous power in the precious blood of Jesus. However, presuppose the blood of Jesus wasn't shed at all, would there still be any level of power in the blood of other creatures that were shed before the crucifixion of Christ? I believe for many, the answer to this question will be a resounding no but let us examine this question critically to see if a yes or a no is the best answer. This is because many in the church circles believe that there is power in the blood of Jesus alone, while all other blood is void of any degree of power, but that's not accurate according to the teachings of the bible.

The answer to this question is yes because other bloods besides the blood of Jesus also commands some degree of power, except that there are limitations to what any other blood besides the blood of Jesus can accomplish. Let us take a critical look at the reason why this is so. The book of Genesis makes us understand that when Cain killed his brother Abel, even though Abel was dead and his lifeless body lay on the ground, his blood spoke from the ground unto God. In this scenario, innocent blood was shed because Abel was killed through no fault of his own. Hence, whatever his blood demanded; God would honor that demand simply because it was the cry of innocent blood. Because Abel's blood demanded vengeance for being murdered by Cain, God answered the demands of the blood of Abel and did exactly what Abel's blood demanded, which was nothing other than vengeance. As a result, not only did God punish Cain for the murder of his brother but Cain was also cursed from the ground and driven out of Eden and from the face of the earth and the face of God to a desolate dwelling place called Nod. This demonstrates the fact that innocent blood has a voice.

It is interesting to note however, that the curse did not come from God. Cain's curse came from the earth. Maybe this is something that you have not paid attention to, but let's go to the scripture that talks about the curse of Cain.

In Genesis 4:11, God said to Cain,

> *And now art thou cursed from the earth, which hath opened her mouth to receive thy brother's blood from thy hand.*

Notice that the curse came from the "earth" and not from God. The reason the earth could curse Cain is because the earth was created by God to be a living thing, not a dead thing. Hence, as a living thing, the earth was forced to open her mouth to receive the innocent blood of Abel, which is something the earth had to do reluctantly because she did not take interest in drinking blood, especially that of the innocent.

Notice also that because the earth is a living thing, and not a dead thing like many Christians had perceived it to be, it is said to have a "mouth," and it is also referred to as "her."

The second example I would like to establish is the fact that there is power to some extent (lesser extent) in other blood besides the blood of Jesus. This is found in 2 Samuel 21:1–14. When King David took over the helm of affairs as king of Israel after the death of Saul, there was a repetitive famine in the land of Israel and David enquired of the Lord about the reason for the famine. In response, the Lord revealed to David that it was because when Saul was king, he had killed several of the Gibeonites with whom Israel had entered a peace covenant dating as far back as the time of Joshua. This account can be found in Joshua 9, which deals with the interlude to the conquest of Canaan.

God guaranteed the nation of Israel victory in that He assured them that no man shall be able to stand before them and that they will be exempted from famine. However once these assurances are violated by any means, Israel will cease to have the security and protection they enjoyed through these promises. Once these covenants are broken, it gives Satan the legal grounds as an adversary to present a case in the court of heaven against Israel.

Therefore, the bible account in II Samuel 21;1-9 illustrated how Satan uses his position as a legal adversary to bring charges in the court of heaven against the people of

God. King Saul in his unrighteous ambition, killed several Gibeonites of whom Israel had entered into a peace covenant dating as far back as the time of Joshua. (Joshua 9). In doing so, King Saul broke the covenant Israel made to protect the Gibeonites. Notice that the covenant Saul broke was instituted 700 years before David and the act that led to the breaking of the covenant was committed by Saul 17 years before David ascended to the throne of Israel. However, when Saul violated the covenant, there was no immediate consequences. There was absolutely no repercussion in the days of Saul. When God made the sun, to stand still upon Gibeon and the Moon, in the valley of Ajalon in the battle of Ajalon, (to create what is known today as a leap year) notice that it was because God was standing up to protect that covenant that Israel had made with the Gibeonites. This shows us the extent to which God respects covenants. This is because that battle at Ajalon was actually the Gibeonites' battle not Israel; but Israel was compelled to intervene as a stronger nation to fight for the Gibeonites because of the existing covenant. However, Saul in his ignorance or arrogance, rose up to go and slaughter the same people whom God had made the sun to stand still for in order for Joshua and his army to fight for and defend.

Notice that Satan did not press charges as a lawyer and adversary during the time of Saul when these atrocities were committed, but rather waited until David, who is a man after God's own heart had taken over the helm of affairs as king over Israel. The reason for the wait is because Satan knew that David is the one chosen by God to make a difference in the life of the people and the nation and bring the people back to God hence it was more strategic in terms of timing to bring charges against Israel during the reign of David. That was when Satan rose up to the court of heaven and decided to bring charges against Israel. In other words, Satan waited for

17 years to pass before he decided to pressed charges against Israel by presenting a case in the courts of heaven against Israel which led to the famine as a punishment.

Notice also that in His capacity as a righteous judge, God could not ignore the charges brought up against Israel. Therefore, God accepted the charges brought against the nation Israel because the jurisdiction of a king covers the entire nation. That explains why the famine that resulted from the charges did not affect the house of Saul only, but rather the entire nation of Israel. Hence the punishment meted was a repetitive famine upon the land, which also became a nation-wide dilemma.

As a result of the famine in the land, David went and enquired of the Lord in order to find out the cause. For a lot of born-again believers when things are happening in our lives, we take it for granted and are not spiritually sensitive enough to take it upon ourselves to go to God and enquire of the Lord. The bible makes it very clear that believers in the New Testament era are a nation of priesthood therefore enquiring from God is a fundamental duty associated with our priesthood. As a born-again believer, when you begin to notice demonic patterns, it should give you a sign that Satan has some legal standing that enables him to perpetuate those patterns in your live or the life of your family. This then calls for the need to enquire of the Lord in order to find out the cause of such demonic patterns. David therefore set himself aside to enquire of the Lord and after it had been revealed to him that the famine was due to a covenant between Israel and the Gibeonites that had been violated by the actions of Saul, David was eager to find a solution and resolution to the matter at hand. He therefore reached out to the Gibeonites and said; what shall I do for you as favor in order for you to bless Israel and stop the curse of famine that's upon the land.

Notice that after the cause has been identified, there are two ways of solving and bringing closure to such situations in the spirit realm.

---

1) By the principle of restitution.
2) By the principle of substitution

(Example - Jesus took our place and became sins for us, so we might become the righteousness of God through Christ).

Hence the moment David received spiritual intelligence about what the cause of the repetitive famine was, he decided to pursue the principle of restitutions by asking the Gibeonites what it is that they would want done in for them in order to appease them and to also reverse the curse. Restitution involves restoring what is lacking so that the grounds that Satan has in the court of heaven can be removed. Watch for demonic patterns like, repetitive miscarriages, untimely deaths, and families in which their women don't get married despite their physical beauty and attraction. The only thing that will change demonic patterns in one's life is when there is a change in the variable that created the pattern.

The bible says "With long life will I satisfy you", meaning that you have a say in your time of exit from this earthly domain. The promise God has given the child of God is based on when you are satisfied with life and not when some evil-minded person wants to take you out of this realm of existence because of their wickedness.

The Gibeonites' satisfaction in this matter was in the death of seven sons of Saul and hence in order to stop the famine, David readily granted their wish and handed over to them, seven sons of Saul to be hanged to death. While the Gibeonites' execution of the seven sons of Saul was violent in its presentation and violent in its proclamation, it had a lesson to teach us about atonement for the ill-doings of humans through the offering of blood. Therefore, notice that immediately after the seven sons of King Saul were identified and hanged to death, the curse of famine ceased. The only reason why they couldn't touch Mephibosheth even though he was a descendent of Saul, was because of the covenant that existed between David and Jonathan who is the father of Mephibosheth. The implication here is that the only reason why the born-again believer is exempted from eternal death is because of the peace covenant between God and humankind that was secured through the eternal blood of the only begotten Son of God who is Jesus the Lamb of God.

This powerful story demonstrates the fact that indeed there is some level of power in blood in general and even in the blood of humans, except that the power that human blood can conjure is limited compared to the blood of the only sinless Lamb of God, who is Jesus Christ. In this story, appeasement was achieved, and the famine ceased because the blood of the seven sons of Saul was shed. I also want to bring to light the fact that the violent nature of the narrative was interrupted by the actions of a mother in mourning. Rizpah a concubine of King Saul, does for her sons in death what she cannot do for them in life—that is, protect their dead bodies from being devoured by predators. Rizpah could not stop King David from taking her sons, and she could not stop the Gibeonites from killing them; however, she did what lay within her power by preventing their bodies from being eaten up by scavengers so she could give them a befitting burial.

In her book *Womanist Midrash*, Wil Gafney paints a vivid portrait of Rizpah's vigil:

> ***Rizpah watches the corpses of her sons stiffen, soften, swell, and sink into the stench of decay ... fights with winged, clawed, and toothed scavengers' night and day. She is there from the spring harvest until the fall rains, as many as six months from Nissan (March/April) to Tishrei (September/October), sleeping, eating, toileting, protecting, and bearing witness.***

That's indeed a powerful example of one woman's dedication to her children even in the face of hopelessness.

There is another striking example in the bible where a plaque ceased immediately human blood was shed. However, note that the human blood was not shed pre-meditatively, since human sacrifices were not permitted by God in the bible. In fact, God cautioned the children of Israel when they entered Canaan, not to pass their children through the fire. A practice done by the Canaanites which was also a human sacrifice. In this incident, it was orchestrated by the grandson of Aaron the High Priest by name Phinehas. It was not premeditated but rather spontaneous and done zealously in honor of God.

Numbers 25:5-13

> 5 *And Moses said unto the judges of Israel, slay ye every one his men that were joined unto Baalpeor.*

> [6] *And, behold, one of the children of Israel came and brought unto his brethren a Midianitish woman in the sight of Moses, and in the sight of all the congregation of the children of Israel, who were weeping before the door of the tabernacle of the congregation.*
>
> [7] *And when Phinehas, the son of Eleazar, the son of Aaron the priest, saw it, he rose from among the congregation, and took a javelin in his hand.*
>
> [8] *And he went after the man of Israel into the tent, and thrust both through, the man of Israel, and the woman through her belly. So the plague was stayed from the children of Israel.*
>
> [9] *And those that died in the plague were twenty and four thousand.*

Notice in the verse five, the disrespect shown to spiritual leadership and authority by the Israelite man in bringing a Midianitish woman into the camp of Israel in the presence of Moses the man of God. This was also at the time during which the children of Israel were weeping before the Lord in repentance at the door of the tabernacle of the congregation so God will spare His people for joining themselves to the worship of Baalpoer the licentious god of the Moabites.

Notice also in the verse seven that as soon as Phinehas, out of jealousy for God, pursued the Israelite man and the Medianitish woman and fatally drove the javelin through their bodies, the plague stopped. This event as well as the example about the killing of the seven sons of King Saul as demanded by the Gibeonites were not done to establish the acceptance of human sacrifices, but rather I cited these examples here to prove that there is some level of power in human blood when it is shed as a means of appeasement. As a result of Phinehas' bravery and his zeal for God, God rewarded him for his action by making an everlasting covenant with Phinehas and his descendants thereafter. Because he turned the wrath of God away from the children of Israel, while he was zealous for the sake of God.

> [10] *And the LORD spake unto Moses, saying,*
>
> [11] *Phinehas, the son of Eleazar, the son of Aaron the priest, hath turned my wrath away from the children of Israel, while he was zealous for my sake among them, that I consumed not the children of Israel in my jealousy.*
>
> [12] *Wherefore say, Behold, I give unto him my covenant of peace:*
>
> [13] *And he shall have it, and his seed after him, even the covenant of an everlasting priesthood; because he was zealous for his God and made an atonement for the children of Israel.*

The power in the blood of Jesus is far more powerful than any other blood could command in that no sin nor guile could be found in Christ Jesus. There is therefore power in every blood, including the blood of bulls, of goats, of turtle doves and even your blood as a human being.

We know the bible says, the blood of bulls and goats could not remove sins, nevertheless we also know that despite this limitation, at least it had power enough to cover sins until another year comes around, which is something that no other fluids like water, oil nor any bodily fluid could accomplish. Notice that the power in other bloods is demonstrated not only in the bible but it is also through demonic sacrifices which always demands the shedding of blood for its' rituals. The fetish priest, satanic cult leader etc., all demands blood for their rituals to invoke demonic powers to work.

My ancestral background is very bloody and messy hence I don't like talking about it except to use it as an example to drive home a point. I originally come from a royal African family. My grandfather was the chief of a warrior tribe in the Eastern Region of Ghana known as the Krobo tribe. If you know much about chieftaincy in any part of the continent of Africa, you would understand that it is all embedded in blood and human sacrifices. This is not something I am proud of; however, I cannot change my human ancestry because that is what I was born into without any choice of mine. But today, I am grateful for the redemptive work of Christ that saved my soul from the pit of hell and from the grip of Satan.

Because divine laws of God are irrefutable, Satan can manipulative them; and for most part, it works for his kingdom of darkness because it's God established system of justice that cannot be changed or revoked.

I remember as a boy of how blood sacrifices were done during almost every traditional ritual and festivity. It took place during installation of chiefs, during annual festivals during the death of a chief, during baby naming ceremony and many more occasions. My ancestral background is so bloody and as ignorant as I was in the early years of my new life in Christ, these spiritual covenants entered in by my ancestors in my bloodline many of whom I never met in person, did affect my spiritual life in Christ severely. I had horrific dreams on numerous occasions where I saw myself sleeping with or having intimacy with some people or creatures that I could not recognize who they were. It was not until later that I understood that I needed to be delivered from the influences of my ancestral bloodline. It was not until through a series of conversations with my dad that I began to understand the implications of some evil covenants upon my life and identify some of the strongholds that I was constantly battling with in my dreams as a new babe in Christ. As a result, I started to stay away from traditional rituals and some cultural practices like the pouring of libation and traditional festivities that I use to think were just ordinary and spiritually harmless. Through the help of God, and knowledge of some matured Christians, I began to deal with these bloodline influences and issues in my Christian life through prayer, fasting and deliverance.

It's worth noting that no one ever enters blood covenant with the devil and his evil forces of darkness and walk away freely simply because they were not physically present when their ancestors made those blood covenants with the powers of darkness.

According to Hebrews 7:5-10 if Levi who was a third generation from Abraham, was present in the loins of Abraham when Abraham paid tithes unto Melchizedek, then make no mistake that you were also present in the loins of your grand-fathers, great grand-fathers, or ancestors when they were making spiritual deals and covenants through blood sacrifices with the forces of darkness. Although they are dead, their blood still runs through your veins today. If you don't believe that, then it means you do not believe the science of genetics and hereditary. For all my teenage and adult life, I have always look like my mother in resemblance both in complexion and most facial features. However, it is so astonishing to me that when I reached the age of 50 years and started growing a lot of gray hair, I began to look more like my father from the look of my hairline, forehead, cheek, and other facial features. Most recently when I stand in front of the mirror, it amazes me the sudden change in my look. Jovially I approached my wife and expressed surprise as to why some genes in my father decided to be dormant in me until I reached the age of 50 years. Where were these genes all along in my teen and young adult years. If I ever doubted the science of genetics, this would be a proof to me that my father's genes were indeed passed on to me through birth.

The loins of Abraham as mentioned in this text simply refers to the bloodline of Abraham or Abraham's DNA in todays' scientific term. Therefore, if Levi was not physically present when Abraham paid tithes unto Melchizedek, yet it is said that he was present through the loins of Abraham, then there is no doubt that I was present, or you were present while centuries ago our ancestors whether ignorantly or not, entered unholy covenants and alliances with the forces of darkness. As much as some Christian may want to ignore it, these things are so real although mystical in nature because it has to do with blood.

This notion can be supported by a powerful statement that Moses the servant of God made in Deuteronomy 29:14-15 when he said.

> *14] Neither with you only do I make this covenant and this oath.*
>
> *15] But with him that standeth here with us this day before the LORD our God, and with him that is not here with us this day:*

The implication here is that, although future generations were not physically present, nevertheless they were present through the blood lineage of those who were physically present at the occasion.

Make no mistake, the lives of the generations that has gone before us, imparts us today in ways beyond explanation or imagination.

The bible says in Lamentations 5:7 "*Our fathers sinned and are no more; and we bear their iniquities".*

Meaning, our ancestors sinned, but they have died, and we the present generation are suffering the punishment they deserved!

Here are some relevant scriptures in the bible that speaks to the fact that we are spiritually connected to the deeds of the generations that has gone before us.

Exodus 20:5

> *You shall not worship them or serve them; for I, the LORD your God, am a jealous God, visiting the iniquity of the fathers on the children, on the*

third and the fourth generations of those who hate Me,

Exodus 34:7

who keeps lovingkindness for thousands, who forgives iniquity, transgression, and sin; yet He will by no means leave the guilty unpunished, visiting the iniquity of fathers on the children and on the grandchildren to the third and fourth generations.

Isaiah 14:21

Prepare for his sons a place of slaughter Because of the iniquity of their fathers. They must not arise and take possession of the earth And fill the face of the world with cities.

Jeremiah 31:29

In those days they will not say again, 'The fathers have eaten sour grapes, And the children's teeth are set on edge.

Jeremiah 32:18

who shows lovingkindness to thousands but repays the iniquity of fathers into the bosom of their children after them, O great and mighty God. The LORD *of hosts is His name.*

Ezekiel 20:4

Will you judge them, will you judge them, son of man? Make them know the abominations of their fathers.

Luke 6:23

Be glad in that day and leap for joy, for behold, your reward is great in heaven. For in the same way their fathers used to treat the prophets.

John 9:2

And His disciples asked Him, Rabbi, who sinned, this man or his parents, that he would be born blind?

Ezekiel 18:19

Yet you say, Why should the son not bear the punishment for the father's iniquity? When the son has practiced justice and righteousness and has observed all My statutes and done them, he shall surely live.

CHAPTER TWO

ENGAGING GOD AS RIGHTEOUS JUDGE

We must understand that God is so vast, that's why the bible has to be so broad in its description of the nature of God. To fully understand the nature of God so we can approach Him effectively in prayer, we will need to find all the different metaphors that's used to describe God. This is necessary because the rules of engagement differ depending on what metaphor is being used to approach God. The move of God that today's church is so desirous of is predicated on our understanding of the nature of God and how to approach and address him correctly in the place of prayer.

Examples;

Luke 11:2 Captures God through the lens or metaphor as a 'father' when it states; "Our Father who art in Heaven". God is seen through the lens of the metaphor – father. Understand that the rules of engagement when we approach God as a father is different from approaching God through the lens of other metaphors that describe God.

Luke 11; 1-9

1 And it came to pass, that, as he was praying in a certain place, when he ceased, one of his disciples said unto him, Lord, teach us to pray, as John also taught his disciples.

2 And he said unto them, When ye pray, say, Our Father which art in heaven, Hallowed be thy name. Thy kingdom come. Thy will be done, as in heaven, so in earth.

3 Give us day by day our daily bread.

4 And forgive us our sins; for we also forgive every one that is indebted to us. And lead us not into temptation; but deliver us from evil.

5 And he said unto them, Which of you shall have a friend, and shall go unto him at midnight, and say unto him, Friend, lend me three loaves;

6 For a friend of mine in his journey is come to me, and I have nothing to set before him?

7 And he from within shall answer and say, Trouble me not: the door is now shut, and my children are with me in bed; I cannot rise and give thee.

> **8 *I say unto you, Though he will not rise and give him, because he is his friend, yet because of his importunity he will rise and give him as many as he needeth.***
>
> **9 *And I say unto you, Ask, and it shall be given you; seek, and ye shall find; knock, and it shall be opened unto you.***

In Luke 11, the verse 9 tells us that it's a parable that captures the believer in our engagement with God in the place of prayer. The metaphor used here in the verse 5 of this context is engaging God as a friend.

> 5 ***And he said unto them, Which of you shall have a friend, and shall go unto him at midnight, and say unto him, Friend, lend me three loaves;***

Notice that there are rules of engagement when one wants to engage God at the level of friendship. Friendship in the spirit then becomes a currency to obtain what one needs from God.

In Luke 18;1 Jesus shows us the design for the creation of men, which is prayer. Hence the child of God is malfunctioning by design if not praying always.

A man that's fainting is a man on life-support. So when you don't pray, Jesus said it mean you are fainting. Therefore, the opposite of being prayerful is not prayerlessness. The opposite of being prayerful according to Jesus, is fainting. Fainting means you are living on life support daily and very soon you will be caving in. Notice therefore that by default, man is a creature of prayer, so if you are getting by through another means; you are only malfunctioning with reference to how you are designed to operate on earth.

Here are a few metaphors used in the bible in relation with Jesus Christ.

Jesus and Metaphors

> **John 6:35:** "I am the bread of life. He who comes to me will never go hungry."
>
> **John 8:12: "I** am the light of the world. Whoever follows me will never walk in darkness, but will have the light of life."
>
> **John 10:11:** "I am the good shepherd. The good shepherd lays down his life for the sheep."
>
> **John 15:5** "I am the true vine; you are the branches. If a man remains in me and I in him, he will bear much fruit."

When Jesus made these statements about himself, he tapped into the power of metaphors. He compared himself to bread, to a shepherd, to light, to a vine because such likeness allowed him to say complex things in a fairly simple manner.

Metaphors - don't just say one thing that can be put into other words; instead, they offer a kind of overflow of additional suggestions and nuances. For example, when Jesus told his disciples that he was a vine and that they were branches, he was making more than one simple point.

1) *A vine and its branches implies an organic relationship, one that changes and grows. Such a metaphor tells us that the disciples' life is not static.*
2) *It also implies a sense of connectedness,*
3) *even a sense of extension. In this manner, Jesus' disciples do not do works of their own power; instead, they must receive strength and ability from the source.*
4) *The metaphor also suggests an extension of appearance: the vine and its branches are one, until a branch is cut off.*

What would happen if we tried to reduce Jesus' meaning to just one of these elements? You would see how much would be lost by reducing it to that sense only?

In a way, metaphors require "thick description". They ask us to take the time to unpack all the subtle possibilities they offer. What the speaker says in a moment, may take us a number of occasions to explore. They are little "texts in miniature" (to quote Ricouer), and like texts, they must be studied and explicated over time to be fully understood. In this sense, metaphors remind us that God's truth is something we live with and continue to explore and continue to grow in. Likewise, they remind us that it takes time and sensitivity to truly understand what someone has said to us.

Luke 18;1

> ***"And he spake † a parable unto them to this end, that men ought always to pray, and not to faint;***

Because in Luke 18;1. We see God in the light of another metaphor; As a judge this time. Jesus is about to present a parable here; and normally the lesson that's supposed to be drawn from a parable is drawn from the end or conclusion of the parable; But in Luke 18; Jesus takes a different course of approach in this parable that has to do with prayer or the act of coming to God with a petition. Jesus here places the lesson before the parable- to show us how urgent he wants us to come to the understanding of what he intend to teach in this parable.

Luke 18:1 this scripture reveals our design.

-*We were design to get by, through prayer*
-*We were design to survive by prayer*
-*We were design to be sustained by prayer*.

That means you ought to pray when you are broke. You ought to prayer when you are sick. You ought to prayer when you are happy or sad. You ought to pray when you are full and when you are empty. You ought to pray whether you are promoted or demoted. Understand that the heavenly realm was created before the earthly realm; the invisible realm was created before the visible realm. Therefore, the visible world derives its existence from the invisible; so if you want to manipulate the visible world; you cannot use the visible to manipulate the visible; you have to manipulate it from the invisible world and that's the role prayer plays in the life of the believer who prays.

Men 'ought;'

δεῖ
'Ought' Means it is an absolute necessity as in a binding situation. It behooves, is right and proper and must needs be done.

It is necessary, there is need of, it behooves,

1. *necessity lying in the nature of the case*
2. *necessity brought on by circumstances or by the conduct of others toward us.*
3. *necessity in reference to what is required to attain some end*
4. *a necessity of law and command, of duty, equity*
5. *necessity established by the counsel and decree of God, especially by that purpose of his which relates to the nature and design of man.*

But many believers have designed their own survival methods and tactics in order to survive without prayer. Any method devised by men in order to survive upon the surface of this earth outside of prayer is a malfunction because it means one is not living according to the original script God designed for man. Note that there is nothing in the Bible called 'prayerlessness'. The opposite of being prayerful is not 'prayerlessness'. It is fainting according to Jesus.

Jesus clearly defined it for us when he said; "***that men ought always to pray, and not faint***"

So you are either praying or fainting. If you are not praying; it means you are living in a state of 'fainting' and that means you can't confront the scepter of darkness when they come against you. So existence without prayer is like existing daily on life support simply because of the fact that you were design to be a creature of prayer.

Luke 18;2 the metaphor in the context is that of God seating as a judge. Not father, a friend or in any other capacity than being a Judge. Luke 18;2 Introduces a metaphor depicting God as a Judge. Notice that although the Judge mentioned in Luke 18:2 is unjust; yet just by pressing, the woman was avenged. But in our case, the God we make appeal to in prayer is a just God, and as such, the way you engage God as a Judge is different from engaging him as a friend or as a father.

This nature and character of God as a Judge is further expanded in **I Peter 5;5-8**

> [5] *Likewise, ye younger, submit yourselves unto the elder. Yea, all of you be subject one to another, and be clothed with humility: for God resisteth the proud, and giveth grace to the humble.*
>
> [6] *Humble yourselves therefore under the mighty hand of God, that he may exalt you in due time:*
>
> [7] *Casting all your care upon him; for he careth for you.*
>
> ***"[8] Be sober, be vigilant; because your adversary the devil, as a roaring lion, walketh about, seeking whom he may devour:***

Peter in this text, is declaring the strategic counsels of God in the verses 5, 6 and 7. These are spiritual counsels are needed in order for the believer to be able to engage in effective spiritual warfare. The verses 5 and 6 reveals the first counsel that has to do with submission and humility. It admonishes the younger to be submissive unto the elder and the verse goes on to reveal that this is an act of humility needed in order for God to grant grace. These days, there is hardly any demarcation between the younger and the elder because many people are trying to rob shoulders with those who are in spiritual authority over them. The verse 7 reveals the second counsel that has to do with casting ones' cares upon the Lord. Note that this is also an act of faith in God.

Finally, the verse 8 calls for the believer to be sober and vigilant, because your adversary like a roaring lion seeking whom he may devour. There is a call to soberness because one can engage better under that condition rather than under excitement. When people are summoned by the court system to appear in response to a law suit, they usually don't go there with excitement. Rather, they appear in soberness of mind and are vigilant, knowing that the circumstances or charges against them has the capability of leading them into jail. Under soberness and vigilance, people are usually able to think through things much better and engage well. Hence one needs these qualities and self-composure in order to engage well and effectively against our adversary the devil.

The word Adversary is very important in this text because it suggest fighting legal charges brought up against the believer in court, and the court in reference here is the court of heaven. Adversary originates from the Greek word ***'antidikos'*** which means an opponent (in a lawsuit); specially Satan who is the Believer's arch-enemy and adversary. It is worth noting that one of the characteristics of the unseen realm is that it is very legalistic and legislative. That is why the Jesus' death on the cross was actually a legal statement to satisfy the claim for divine justice in the realm of the spirit where God seats as the judge of all and where Satan presents himself as an adversary and a lawyer to present accusations against the born-again believer.

So Satan in this text, is not just an opponent. The right description for his role is a legal opponent in a law suit. This is how Satan operates as a lawyer or an adversary to bring accusations against the believer in the court of heaven. Many believers are carrying bondages that are under legal domain and unless their deliverance is carried out legally they are not going to experience total deliverance from these bondages. Although the believer is justified through the blood of Jesus, note that justification is only associated with legal matters and scenarios. Justification in a judicial register means to be discharged and acquitted.

Hebrews 12;22-24

> [22] *But ye are come unto mount Sion, and unto the city of the living God, the heavenly Jerusalem, and to an innumerable company of angels,*
>
> [23] *To the general assembly and church of the firstborn, which are written in heaven, and to God the Judge of all, and to the spirits of just men made perfect,*
>
> [24] *And to Jesus the mediator of the new covenant, and to the blood of sprinkling, that speaketh better things than that of Abel.*
>
> [25] *See that ye refuse not him that speaketh. For if they escaped not who refused him that spake on earth, much more shall not we escape, if we turn away from him that speaketh from heaven:*

Hebrews 12 gives us the infrastructure of the composition of the court of heaven. All the things mentioned here are present in the court of heaven. Now watch the location; Mt Zion that's the city of the God who is alive is described as the location. Satan said "I will ascend to Zion. In so doing he wanted to become the Administrator of Zion, the city of the living God with the goal to be equal with God.

Psalm 48:1-14

1 Great is the LORD, and greatly to be praised in the city of our God, in the mountain of his holiness.

2 Beautiful for situation, the joy of the whole earth, is mount Zion, on the sides of the north, the city of the great King.

3 God is known in her palaces for a refuge.

4 For, lo, the kings were assembled, they passed by together.

5 They saw it, and so they marvelled; they were troubled, and hasted away.

6 Fear took hold upon them there, and pain, as of a woman in travail.

7 Thou breakest the ships of Tarshish with an east wind.

8 As we have heard, so have we seen in the city of the LORD of hosts, in the city of our God: God will establish it for ever. Selah.

9 We have thought of thy lovingkindness, O God, in the midst of thy temple.

> [10] *According to thy name, O God, so is thy praise unto the ends of the earth: thy right hand is full of righteousness.*
>
> [11] *Let mount Zion rejoice, let the daughters of Judah be glad, because of thy judgments.*
>
> [12] *Walk about Zion, and go round about her: tell the towers thereof.*
>
> [13] *Mark ye well her bulwarks, consider her palaces; that ye may tell it to the generation following.*
>
> [14] *For this God is our God for ever and ever: he will be our guide even unto death.*

There is a place in Christ that we as believers are seated. It is only from that place that we are at a vantage point over Satan. According to Hebrews 12:22, the court of heaven is also a pavilion of numerous company of angels. The angels' assignment in this court is the keeping of records.

Hebrews 12:22

> [22] *But ye are come unto mount Sion, and unto the city of the living God, the heavenly Jerusalem, and to <u>an innumerable company of angels,</u>*

So when a case is raised, all the angels that work on that case will have to be present in the court of heaven. (This is unlike human court where files can get missing and a case dismissed without going through proper proceedings of the law). Therefore, when one is invoking remembrance on a certain matter, the angels that are in charge of those records will be present as witnesses.

Hebrews 12:23

> *"To the general assembly and church of the firstborn, which are written in heaven, and to God the Judge of all, and to the spirits of just men made perfect"*

To God the judge of all.

Jesus the mediator of the covenant. His voice is heard in the court of heaven as well. He seats as an Advocate in the court of heaven. In the court of heaven, the blood of sprinkling is not a thing. It's a voice, because it's the blood of sprinkling that speaks better things on behalf of the born-again believer in Christ. The blood of sprinkling is the instrument through which we can obtain mercy at the court of heaven.

'Come boldly to the throne of grace, that Ye May obtain mercy..."

Note that without grace, we cannot find mercy in the court of heaven.

CHAPTER THREE

WHAT MAKES BLOOD UNIQUE

Considering the foundation laid in the previous chapter, what is it about blood that makes it so powerful? What is it about blood that even in death, it is able to negotiate resolutions for appeasement, in some cases providing physical covering (as in the case of Adam and Eve in the garden of Eden); in some cases providing a temporal spiritual covering (as in the era of Old Testament temple sacrifices offered with the blood of bulls and goats) and in the case of Jesus' crucifixion, death, burial and resurrection, providing the ultimate removal of sin. What is it about blood that makes it so effective as a medium for covenants and sacrifices? Why not water or oil or some other bodily fluid, but blood.

What is it about blood that once it begins to bleed out of ones' body, one begin to feel dizzy, weak, lose consciousness, leading to the ultimate death.

What is it about blood that its intrinsic characteristics can be passed on endlessly from one generation to another even though the people who passes it on no longer exist, yet every characteristic and intricate details of their blood remains intact in their descendants.

Does this matchless power in the blood as compared to any other fluid has anything to do with the fact that blood is red in color as in humans? There are certain groups or religious denominations that do believe that the power in blood in general and particularly the blood of Jesus is because of its red coloration. As a result, some members of these groups or denominations would usually wear red attires on Easter or during special spiritual events. What if blood in general wasn't red at all but blue, or green or some other color. Would it still command the power and significance it does.? Let's examine whether the red coloration of blood has any impact on the power that blood commands.

Blood Colors

Let us begin by examining what gives humans, other mammals, and most creatures the red coloration in their blood.

Red Blood

The blood of humans and other mammals is red because it contains a compound known as hemoglobin, which is a complex protein molecule in blood cells. Hemoglobin by its composition is rich in iron. The iron in hemoglobin reacts with the oxygen content in blood, giving blood its red coloration. This chemical reaction is like when iron as an element reacts with oxygen to give rust its reddish-brown color, which in a way looks very much like blood in color. This means that if there wasn't the presence of iron in hemoglobin, the blood in humans, other mammals and some creatures wouldn't be red in color at all. However, it is common knowledge that there are a few exceptions to creatures with red blood.

Blue Blood

There are some creatures that bleed blue blood. O yes there are, and if you observe closely you would come to that realization. Some types of octopus, squid, and crustaceans have blue blood and the processes involved in the blue coloration of their blood is like that in humans and other mammals except that their bodies contain high concentration of copper instead of iron in man and mammals. When the copper comes into contact and reacts with oxygen, it gives their blood a blue coloration instead of red.

Green Blood

There are other creatures that bleed green instead of red or blue. Some types of lizards, for example the skink lizard has green blood due to a buildup of greenish chemicals called biliverdin which are by-products of the liver. The human body also produces biliverdin to some extent, however it is excreted through facies as waste product of the liver. However, with the lizards, the biliverdin produces the green coloration in their blood since their anatomy is not as advance as mammals to excrete this chemical out of their bodies.

The conclusion that one can draw from the different colorations of the blood of different creatures is that the power of blood in general has no dependency on the color of a creatures' blood. This therefore leads us to the conclusion that the power in blood is color-blind. Notice that there is nowhere in the bible that it is said or stated that the blood of bulls and goats or that of Jesus Christ the sinless lamb of God, was able to accomplish the things they did accomplish simply because of its red coloration.

The power that different types of blood commands is independent on the color of blood, hence it would be safe to conclude that the power in blood of any sort is color blind.

Source of Power in Blood

According to Leviticus 17:11a - The source of power in the blood comes from the fact that God, in His infinite wisdom decided to hide the life of the flesh (any flesh) in its blood.

Leviticus 17:11a states, "*For the life of the flesh is in the blood and I have given it to you upon the altar to make atonement for your souls; for it is the blood that makes atonement*".

It's interesting to note that blood is so powerful to the extent that nothing can stand in the way of blood or obstruct the flow of blood including blood itself.

That's why when one develops blood clot his or her life is in danger because blood clot simply means blood in its solid state is trying to stand in the way of the flow of blood as a liquid. Therefore, the reason why blood is so powerful is because life lives in blood and not in the flesh. Hence it totally makes sense to say that the residential address of life, is blood.

Also, because life lives in blood, blood then becomes a representation of the quality of life of any flesh. Hence there are levels of power that the blood of any animal or flesh can invoke or command. This explains why under the Old Testament sacrificial laws and ordinances, at times blood of different animals were required for sacrifice for different reasons. Notice that in the Old Testament era, at times and under certain circumstances, the blood of turtle doves were required for appeasement sacrifices. Sometimes the blood of goats were required, and yet at other times the blood of bulls and heifers became necessary instead of the blood of goats. In the case of the example cited earlier that involved the appeasement for the Gibeonites whose forefathers were unjustly murdered by King Saul, the blood of the seven sons of Saul became the requirement for appeasement in ordain other to stop the famine that was upon the land. Although under normal circumstances human sacrifices were not acceptable practice among the people of God, but in this unique circumstance, because it was demanded by the Gibeonites who Jews were not, the blood of humans (the seven sons of king Saul) was offered for appeasement. The final atonement offered using human blood was that of God Himself through Jesus Christ the sinless lamb of God.

2 Corinthians 5:19 declares; "*God was in Christ, reconciling the world unto himself; not imputing their trespasses unto them*".

This is the reason why at times when people of the world consult fetish priest or other agents of the powers of darkness, demand is made for the blood of chicken, and at times the blood of goats or even that of human beings have been required in some cases. This is because different blood command different levels of power. That is why the bible says the blood of Jesus spoke better things than the blood of Abel. The blood of Jesus was better in volume, better in quality, and better in vocabulary of expression.

The death of Christ to secure the eternal salvation of humankind is a mystery beyond human comprehension. God cannot die because He is eternal Spirit however, because Christ died in the flesh, God also died in Christ and that is a mystery.

According to the Old Testament culture and practices, the Ark, which was made of wood, emphasized the person of Jesus or to put it in a more precise way, His humanity and the Mercy seat emphasized the purpose of Christ. The Mercy Seat was a plate of pure gold and had no wood. Meaning nothing but deity could offer saving mercy. In all the universe, there was no moral, sinless blood to be found except that of the sinless Lamb of God. All human blood is immoral because of sin and the blood of animals are non-moral, therefore it is not possible that the blood of bulls and of goats should take away sins. Hence the sin debt had to be paid with heaven's currency, which is nothing than the blood of the sinless Lamb of God.

According to Hebrews 9:13-14

> *13] For if the blood of bulls and of goats, and the ashes of an heifer sprinkling the unclean, sanctifieth to the purifying of the flesh:*
>
> *14] How much more shall the blood of Christ, who through the eternal Spirit offered himself without spot to God, purge your conscience from dead works to serve the living God?*

In the above scripture, notice that the writer is comparing the life potency in the blood of different creatures. It mentions the blood of bulls and of goats as well as the blood of Christ. This can be likened unto comparing the potency in different drugs or vitamins. However, it is worth noticing that the writer is also comparing the lasting effect in terms of how long the power in a particular blood can sustain appeasement.

What many people don't realize is that blood is currency in the realm of the spirit by which transactions are conducted. This explains why the blood of Jesus was able to purchase our redemption.

Hebrews 10:3-4

> *3] But in those sacrifices there is a remembrance again made of sins every year.*
>
> *4] For it is not possible that the blood of bulls and of goats should take away sins.*

In the days of old, the mercy seat is where God met with Moses (Exodus 25:22) and according to Numbers 7:89, it is from the mercy seat that was upon the ark that Moses heard the voice of one speaking unto him. The Mercy Seat typifies Christ and hence it is the place where "mercy and truth are met together; and righteousness and peace have kissed each other" (Psalm 85:10). Although Christ was God's sinless Lamb, even so no one is saved by the perfect life of Christ if He did not die to shed His blood because redemption rests on His atoning death only and nothing else.

The conception and virgin birth of Christ is a mystery. Since life lives in blood, the life of God came into blood so it can be implanted as a seed in the womb of a virgin named Mary. The seed then grew and turned into a man called Jesus and His blood was ultimately shed for atonement of the sins of humanity on Calvary's wooden cross. This is a beautiful picture of how God became flesh for the sake of dying for the atonement of the sins of humans. This is because a currency is that which has purchasing power, and so do all blood and especially the efficacious blood of Jesus because it was able to purchase our redemption from the bondage of sin and Satan unto His marvelous light. Moreover, anything that has purchasing power can be used to conduct transactions, and so did the blood of Jesus transact on our behalf the freedom from sin that we did not deserve to have but needed to live.

I Corinthians 6:20 states, "*For ye are purchased with a price: therefore, glorify God in your body*". What was the currency that was used to conduct that purchase. It is nothing but the blood of Jesus.

Also, according to I Peter 1:18-19.

> *18] Forasmuch as ye know that ye were not redeemed with corruptible things, as silver and gold, from your vain conversation received by tradition from your fathers.*
>
> *19] But with the precious blood of Christ, as of a lamb without blemish and without spot:*

This explains why transactions and covenants are conducted in the spirit realm through blood and in case you have forgotten what that's called – it is the term known as redemption. Therefore, when one speaks about the shedding blood they are speaking about the giving up of life. The reason why in the Old Testament, God forbid Israel from eating the blood of animals is because it's tantamount to eating the life of another creature. Meanwhile notice that the eating of the flesh of the same creature wasn't a problem at all or of any concern to God because the life of the creature does not dwell in its flesh but rather in its' blood.

Before I close this chapter, there are a few things I would like to mention about blood.

1. *Life of every creature is in the blood of the creature.*
2. *All healing is in the blood since the component that heals things in the body is in the blood.*
3. *All nutrients needed by the body are in blood.*
4. *All protection needed by the body is in the blood that's why the white blood cells serves as immune system to the body to fight off diseases.*

5. *All sustenance is in the blood. We are all living with a transfused blood through Christ because the blood of Adam our first human ancestor was contaminated and polluted by sin.*
6. *Every disease in the body can be traced in the blood, so when one eats blood, they are literally eating diseases that may be present in a creature. That's why God forbid the children of Israel not to eat the blood of animals.*
7. *All death is only possible in blood- that's why they do blood test to see what's going on in your body. When one takes in a poisonous substance, it goes into the blood stream first before it becomes detrimental or its' fatal impart is felt by the body.*

Notice that all other organs in the body exist for the sole function of serving the blood. For instance, the job of the liver is to purify the blood, the kidney serve the blood, the heart exist only to pump the blood and so is the bile which exist to serve the blood by dealing with poisonous and toxic substance introduced into the blood stream. All these vital organs exist to serve the blood because it is the blood that host the life-giving component. Hence blood is the live wire of the body and not the heart, kidney, liver, or any other organ in the body.

Hence if you want to kill a creature the easiest and fastest way to do so is by getting directly to the blood because that's where life lives. That's why people when they want to kill others, try to stab them, shoot them, or inflict their bodies with some form of weapon that could cause blood to drain out of the body of the victim. They do this to directly attack the blood stream, just like a poison or some form of toxic substances would attack the blood stream directly to cause harm and danger to the life of the victim. Notice that the goal of inflicting a fatal wound to the body is to puncture the body to get to the blood. That's exactly what poison also does to the body. Before it gets to any vital organ of the body, poisons first attacks the blood stream directly and once it overpowers the blood; all other organs succumb and become victims of poisonous attacks. This underscores the important role of blood in the body, not forgetting the fact that countless lives are saved daily through direct blood transfusion in our hospitals and medical facilities. That's why during the crucifixion the Roman soldiers had to punch Jesus's body to get to His blood so to ensure He dies faster. It was the most horrific death one could ever go through, but Christ Jesus endured it for the salvation of humankind. Hence the Prophet Isaiah in Isaiah 53 declared.

"***when ye shall see him, there is no beauty that ye shall desire of him, a man of sorrow, acquainted with grieve.***

Blood of bulls and goat couldn't take away sin. God had to kill a man and that man ought to be an Adam for a perfect exchange to be accomplished because sin was introduced through the first and physical Adam in the garden of Eden. Therefore, while there is a first Adam and the last Adam, notice that there is no other Adam in-between and none after Jesus who represent the last Adam. All ended with Jesus as the final and ultimate sacrifice for sin. I Corinthians 15:45-47 says, the first Adam was of the flesh, but the last Adam was a life-giving spirit.

The Lamb of God

For 4000 years and more of human history, everybody dragged their lamb to offer as sacrifice unto God, but after a long while, God said I'm going to produce my own lamb, that's why when John the Baptist saw Jesus coming to his baptism, he said of Jesus;

"Behold the Lam of God that taketh away the sin of the world'.

Although John was related to Jesus in the flesh, but John said;

---

for I knew him not; but he that send me to be baptized is the same that said he will show me the one.

So, John and Jesus are cousins, but John didn't know that his earthly cousin was the one who would come to die and redeem humankind from their sins.

Notice that in the days of old, only people with guilt brought lamb for the sacrifice for their sins. But although God is without sin nor guilt, yet He brought his own lamb to take care of our sins. Since Adam's sin was passed on to all humanity and caused humanity's blood to be polluted, it meant we needed somebody who has a blood that hasn't been contaminated with sin to give us a blood transfusion so the life of God would come back into humankind for humankind to live again spiritually.

When Adam sinned, sin didn't attack his liver, pancreas, heart or kidney. Sin went straight to his blood and polluted not only the blood of Adam but also that of all descendants of Adam because it's only through blood that Adam's sin could be passed on to pollute the rest of the human family.

Lev 17; tells us that the life of an animal is in the blood and since animals cannot sin and their blood is not polluted; that's why God says in Leviticus 17 that He has given it to us as a temporal means to atone for our sins until the appointed time when the permanent sacrifice could be made through the blood of Jesus the sinless lamb of God and through Calvary to permanently redeem man.

Also, it is worth noting that since life is in blood, diseases of all sorts dwells in blood and that's why God told Israel not to eat blood. But several centuries later, Jesus said to his audience, you could drink of my blood and eat of my flesh, and although it was symbolic in meaning and not literal, this He said because his blood was not contaminated. The blood of Jesus was pure in every sense of the word. His blood contained all the nutrients and life but the one from all others contains diseases. No matter how good a man is or can be, since he is born of a woman and the seed of a man, one cannot trust their life on another person's life. Notice also that when Adam and Eve sin, they sowed fig leaves together and cover themselves, but there is no blood in leaves so God had to kill an animal which is a way to cover them with blood temporally until the eternal blood of Christ was shed.

With Cain and Abel sacrifice, Cain's sacrifice was rejected because it's impossible for one to approach God without blood. Cain who didn't go to God with blood represent all the other religions of the world that attempts to approach God without doing so through the efficacious blood of Jesus. According to Leviticus 14 in the days of temple worship and sacrifices, the priest couldn't go before God without blood on earlobes, big toes, and other parts of the body as a way of purification and sanctification. The same applies to us today. For without the blood of Jesus that was shed for our sins, we wouldn't have been able to approach God nor stand in His presence, because we can only see God through Christ as our lens. This therefore reminds me of the reason why God had to hide Moses in the cliff of the rock, when Moses demanded to see God's face. The rock became the lens and the only means through which Moses could see God and not die because that rock is Jesus.

CHAPTER FOUR

THE UNBELIEVABLE REPORT

Being in heaven before and knowing the divine justice system of God, Satan knew too well that if he can get man to sin against God, the irrefutable laws of God's divine system of justice that says *"the soul that sinneth, it shall die"* would apply to humankind and as a result man's sins would bring upon him judgement and eternal condemnation. Satan also knew that after he has been able to get man to sin man would plunge into eternal condemnation and his soul will be lost for good. As a result, the only way to redeem man would be through the shedding of blood without which there can be no remission of sins.

Furthermore, Satan knew too well that God is not man and hence there would never be any possibility at all for God to become man to redeem the fallen man from the state of eternal damnation. Therefore, in the garden of Eden, Satan came at Adam and Eve with all he has got to cause man to fall to disobedience of God's instructions and to ultimately sin against God through disobedience. Satan eventually succeeded and that began the story of man's eternal doom and damnation.

However, Satan was totally in hindsight of the all-sufficient power of God to become anything He chooses to become without having to break His own rules set forth before the foundations of the world. Hence the great Apostle Paul captured this gross ignorance on the part of Satan when through the revelation of the Spirit of God, he wrote in I Corinthians 2:7-8.

7] But we speak the wisdom of God in a mystery, even the hidden wisdom, which God ordained before the world unto our glory:

8] Which none of the princes of this world knew: for had they known it, they would not have crucified the Lord of glory.

Satan was ignorant of the fact that the God of the universes could stoop so low and condescend to the low estate of fallen man, to the extent of becoming man to appease for the sins of humankind.

This is what the prophesy of Isaiah was referring to when in Isaiah 53 the prophet through the inspiration of the spirit of God pose the question, "***Who has believed our report***".

What he was trying to say was that, if it was to be told to men and to entire creation that the great creator God put on flesh in the form of a man, who would ever believe that report. The continuation of this prophesy however says, "*And to whom is the arm of the Lord revealed*". Meaning, that whosoever believes that "unbelievable report" of God's incarnation as the man Christ Jesus and the fact that the great creator God put on flesh and became man to redeem man, to them shall the arm of the Lord would be revealed. The reference to the arm of the Lord is in reference to our salvation. That's why the bible declares that whosoever shall call upon the name of the Lord shall be saved. That refers to salvation through the mighty arm of the Lord, hence all the sinner needs to do, is to believe the unbelievable report that the great creator became our Savior, yet all of God's fullness still dwells in Him. As a result of believing a report that is so far fetch from the realm of human possibilities, salvation would be made available for the sinner.

This I believe is what prompted William E. Booth-Clibborn to pen the words of the popular hymn "Down from His Glory" The word of this beautiful hymn is as follows,

---

Down from His glory
Ever living story,
My God and Savior came,
Born in a manger.
To His own a stranger)
A man of sorrows, tears, and agony

REFRAIN.
O how I love Him! How I adore Him!
My breath, my sunshine, my all in all.
The great Creator became my Savior.
And all God's fullness dwellers in Him

In my opinion, this song is a beautiful masterpiece which embodies as well as captures a well-rounded and complete revelation of the theology of the godhead for the following reasons listed below.

Down from His glory - ***speaks of God's sovereignty.***

Ever living story - ***speaks of the gospel of Jesus Christ.***

My God and Savior came - ***speaks of Christ's divinity.***

Born in a manger -***speaks of Christ's humanity and humility.***

To His own a stranger - ***speaks of His rejection***

A man of sorrows, tears, and agony - ***speaks of Christ's suffering and crucifixion.***

It All Began in Eden

The bible records in Genesis 5:2 that,

***"Male and female* created *he them*; and blessed *them*, and *called* their *name Adam*, in the day when they were created".**

"He called their name Adam" implies that Adam is a plural word hence all of us are Adam as we are all direct descendants of Adam and Eve. The word Adam means that which is earthy and so are we. That also explains why when the first Adam sinned, his sins were imputed upon all the other Adam(s) which is humanity in its entirety.

The bible also declares that after the fall of man, God spoke to Adam and said unto him, *"Where art thou"*. Notice that God knows everything and knows where everything is at, yet God ask Adam, "where art thou". Why this question if indeed God knows all things?

It is worth mentioning that "where art thou." had nothing to do with Adam's physical location or topography, but rather it was about Adam's disposition which had

to do with the condition of his heart after the fall.

As a result of man's disobedience, he lost his position with God and with heaven. Hence Isaiah 63 says that through Adam, every one of us became like sheep gone astray from the rulership of heaven. Note also that the word 'Sin' does not just apply to stealing, lying, fornication, malice, and all that we know to be sinful. The root word for sin is the word *rebellion* which simply means coming against or an uprising against a ruling government or authority, and hence the consequence or wages of sin or rebellion became spiritual death in humankind.

When God caused a deep sleep to fall upon Adam, He opened Adam's side, took out a rib, and from it, He formed a wife for Adam. Now Adam is the figure of him that was to come (Romans 5:14) and Eve typifies the church that's mentioned in Ephesians 5:30-32. Adam's deep sleep typified the death of Christ. The opening of Adam's side is a foreshadow of the piercing of Jesus' side, from which came blood and water. That is how Jesus obtained His bride, the Church. He purchased her with His own blood and sanctified her with the washing of water by the word of God (Ephesians 5:26). Moreover, "rivers of living water" spoke of the spirit which they that believe on Christ should receive, however notice that the blood is mentioned first before the water, because no one can receive the spirit until they have personally appropriated the blood of Christ to their own heart and life. Therefore, they who have applied the blood and whom the Holy Spirit indwells and governs are the true Church that Christ came to purchase.

O' Death, where is thy Sting

Death existed before it had power to kill. Contrary to what many believe, death was not created by Satan and neither does Satan has power over death. Death was created by God hence notice that in the book of Revelation, it was God who was commanding 'death' and instructing 'death' on what to do when death appeared riding on a pale horse. It was God who was giving to death its assignment to be accomplished.

Revelation 6:8

And I looked, and behold a pale horse: and his name that sat on him was Death, and Hell followed with him. And power was given unto them over the fourth part of the earth, to kill with sword, and with hunger, and with death, and with the beasts of the earth.

Contrary to what many Christians believe, "Death" was not created by Satan. Death existed before the fall but did not have power to kill. The sting of death was enacted by God only after man had sinned and fell short of the glory of God.

According to this text, "death" took his instructions directly from God and not Satan. So, one would wonder why the good and merciful God would create such a thing as death. But notice that although death was in existence, but death could not kill nor was death given the power to kill. This is because death had no sting until it was given permission to kill after Adam and Eve sinned in the garden.

How do we know this? Because God said to Adam in Genesis 2:17

***But of the tree of the knowledge of good and evil,* thou shalt *not eat of it: for in the day that thou eatest thereof* thou shalt surely die.**

Meaning death already existed when God was giving Adam this instruction, however, death did not have the power to kill until the day Adam disobeyed the instruction God had given. Hence the power of death was enacted after the fall of man and not before. So, sin and rebellion enacted the power of death according to I Corinthians 15: 54-57

> [54] *So when this corruptible shall have put on incorruption, and this mortal shall have put on immortality, then shall be brought to pass the saying that is written, Death is swallowed up in victory.*
>
> [55] *O death, where is thy sting? O grave, where is thy victory?*
>
> [56] *The sting of death is sin; and the strength of sin is the law.*
>
> [57] *But thanks be to God, which giveth us the victory through our Lord Jesus Christ.*

The 54th verse makes us understand that someday death shall be swallowed up in victory. This means that there is going to be a time when death would lose its sting and would be stripped of its power to kill. The same sting it gained in the garden as the result of the sin of man through disobedience is going to be taken away from death one day. Although those who die without Christ shall still be subject to the power of death, true believers in Jesus Christ would not because they have no covenant with death. The covenant of the true believer is with life and not death, that why death would not be able to have power over the believer beyond the grave. The 55th verse exposes to us the source of power that death has. This comes from the fact that death gained its power through man's disobedience. Without the sting, death had no spiritual power over humankind. It is just like the scorpion or other venomous creatures like the snake. What makes scorpion or some snakes deadly is their sting. Other than their sting, they would have been as harmless and powerless as any similar reptiles or creature that belong to the same spices. According to the same verse, the sting of death is identified as sin, which is in turn empowered or fueled by the law because sinful man could not measure up to the demands of the law hence became even more sinful.

Romans 5:12 *Therefore, just as sin entered the world through one man, and death through sin, and in this way, death came to all people, because all sinned.*

Death was created as a servant to serve the purposes of God; however, it was given power to kill only after the fall of man. Hence for the true believer who has been redeemed by the blood of Jesus Christ, death will remain a servant who will carry true believers to their eternal home. But for the unbeliever, death will rather be a master that

> ***will exercise its power and sting over the unbeliever through eternal death in hell fire.***

This is why it's worth noting that the sacrifice of Christ on Calvary, accomplished two-fold requirements of God.

- *Christ died to save man from eternal condemnation.*
- *Christ also died to fulfill the demands of the law that man could not fulfill, by nailing it to the cross.*

Finally, the 57th verse of I Corinthians 15, establishes a very important fact about the eternal security of the soul of man and for every soul that ever lived and would ever live upon the surface of the earth. It states that the victory over the sting of death is only possible through our Lord Jesus Christ. What this means is that, outside Christ Jesus, death would still be able to exercise its sting over all those who reject salvation through Christ Jesus.

Romans 5:17

> *"17 For if, by the trespass of the one man, death reigned through that one man, how much more will those who receive God's abundant provision of grace and of the gift of righteousness reign in life through the one man, Jesus Christ!"*

According to Revelation 12, Satan who is the accuser of the brethren was watching all this enfold in the garden, and the moment man sinned through disobedience by eating of the forbidden fruit, the devil started to rail accusations before God against man because the devil knows that death is the penalty for sin. The devil also knowing the nature of God, was certain that God will not back down on his own laws because God is faithful by His nature. So, man's disobedience and the consequent penalty for that disobedience was like "I got you" moment for the devil because now, the devil could say, "God if you are indeed the faithful God you claim to be and I know you to be, then your masterpiece who is the man you created has sin so be faithful to your own laws and let death reign eternally in man's body and soul because the wages God had proposed for sin is death."

Also, since in the garden of Eden, Satan has been on a high alert while watching the history of humanity unfold through the ages because a prophesy was left as far back in the garden of Eden that ***"the seed of the woman shall bruise the head of the serpent"***. Hence Satan knows too well that according to this prophesy there is coming a day when the last Adam will come, who would be a danger to the dominion and authority Satan stole away from the first Adam in the garden of Eden. So, in the process of time came John the baptizer, as the forerunner of Jesus Christ in the wilderness of Judea.

Everything about John seem misunderstood for lack of clarity of who he truly is and what his core mission was supposed to be. In terms of his identity, they called him Elias; but he was not really the prophet Elijah since no two persons can be the same.

John the Baptist's involvement in baptism was only to serve as a mechanism to help him identify as well as reveal the Christ (the anointed one) to the people of his time.

John only came in the spirit and power of Elijah. Also, in terms of his mission, they referred to him as John the Baptizer but baptizing people in the waters of the river Jordan was not really his mission. Jesus testified of him saying; ***"what do you go to the desert to see? A Prophet, indeed".*** Therefore, John was a prophet according to Jesus' own words. He was the last of the Old Testament line of prophets and the first of the New Testament line of Prophets. A 'sandwich prophet' between the two testaments as one would call him. Notice however that John's involvement in baptism was not his key mission. His involvement in baptism was only to serve as a 'mechanism' to help him identify as well as reveal the Christ the anointed one to his fellow countrymen and the people of his dispensation. This is because it was revealed to John by the spirit of God that; ***"upon whosoever he will see the spirit descend upon like a dove, he was the one to come; the Christ."***

John 1:31.

> ***And I knew him not: but that he should be made manifest to Israel, therefore † am I come baptizing with water.***

Therefore, I believe that as John engaged in his baptism ministry, he had his eyes opened to ensure that he does not miss the moment of this revelation of the Christ, the anointed one sent from God. Therefore, as soon as Jesus came to the wilderness to be baptized of John and John observed the sign that has been given to him by the spirit as an identifier of who the Christ will be, John immediately announced Jesus as *"The Lamb of God that taketh away the sins of the world"* and from the very moment and onwards, Satan set his face like a flint to go after Jesus.

The Passion of the Christ

Notice that it was only Mary and the beloved disciple of Jesus called John who were closest to the cross of Jesus at the time of His crucifixion but not Joseph nor any other male and female figure. This is because Jesus had gone on the cross to fulfill something that does not involve the seed of an earthly father hence God would have it that Joseph will be taken out of the picture even before that day comes since his presence was not a necessity in the fulfillment of what Christ Jesus was about to accomplish on the cross of Calvary.

The reason why Jesus' death on the cross is referred to as "the passion of the Christ" is because it can the liken unto the passion that result in an intercourse between husband and wife.

Jesus went on the cross to fulfill our spiritual new birth which has nothing to do with a male father, nor a male seed. However, notice that the new birth had everything to do with a mother figure because as far as the earthly realm is concern, women are the gateway to birth and life. It also had something to do with a son who in this case was represented by the presence of the beloved disciple John because the product of the spiritual new birth gives us the right to sonship. That is why on the cross, Jesus turned to His mother Mary and said, ***"Mother behold thy Son"***; and to John, he said; ***"Son Behold thy mother."***

According to Romans 5;12. Says; *Wherefore, † as by one man sin entered into the world, and death by sin; and so, death passed upon all men, for that all have sinned.*

The implication here is that the power of death was made potent through blood. In other words, death obtained its power to be passed on from one man Adam to all men through blood. Therefore, the blood in you is far older than you. As a matter of fact, you got here on earth through a blood that already existed because the blood was there before you came. Meaning the blood in your father, grandfather, and great grandfather and for that matter, your ancestors flows through your veins and is still part of who you are. Except you don't believe in the science of genetics and hereditary. That's why Joseph couldn't take part in the birth of Christ. Otherwise, his blood would have contaminated the blood of the sinless lamb of God. Notice therefore that there was no problem with Jesus having an earthly biological mother because it was a possibility for Mary to carry Jesus without the nature of man corrupting the baby that would be born from the womb of Mary.

Women don't produce seed; their womb only serve as the soil or fertile grounds into which the seed of the male man can be planted.

However, there would have been a big problem if Joseph was to partake in the birth of Jesus genetically because it is the blood of the man that produces the offspring- That's call seed. That would have meant Jesus' birth would have been inseminated by a corruptible seed and hence Jesus couldn't be a sinless lamb of God. Therefore, although Jesus was born in a human body, however He did not originate from the seed of a mortal man because the Holy Spirit stepped in to play that role. That's why the angel of the Lord who announced the birth of Christ to Mary in Luke 1:35-38 (NKJV)

And the angel answered and said to her, "The Holy Spirit will come upon you, and the power of the Highest will overshadow you; therefore, also, that Holy One who is to be born will be called the Son of God.

So, although Jesus came in a human body, however Jesus' blood was a representation of the life of God in flesh.

First and Last Adam

Notice the bible speaks of the first Adam but with no mention to a 'third or fourth Adam' but rather to Jesus as the last Adam. Meaning that after Jesus there would be no need for a third, fourth or fifth Adam in that Jesus is the epitome and the one who crowns the eternal salvation plan of God.

1 Corinthians 15:45-49
(New International Version)

> [45] *So it is written: The first man Adam became a living being"*[a]*; the last Adam, a life-giving spirit.* [46] *The spiritual did not come first, but the natural, and after that the spiritual.*

1 Corinthians 15:21-22

> *For since death came through a man, the resurrection of the dead comes also through a man. 22 For as in Adam all die, so in Christ all will*

> *be made alive. 23 But each in turn: Christ, the firstfruits; then, when he comes, those who belong to him.*

When the first Adam sinned in the garden of Eden, the spirit of God left Him in the garden. Thousands of years after that came Jesus, as the last Adam also in a garden called Gethsemane, praying and sweating drops of blood and crying in tears unto his heavenly father.

Luke 22;44 ***And being in an agony he prayed more earnestly: and his sweat was as it were great drops of blood falling down to the ground.***

This is because at that point in the garden of Gethsemane, the spirit of God departed from Jesus who is the last Adam just like the Spirit of the Lord departed from the first Adam. That's what the psalmist saw in the prophecy in Psalm 51 when he said, ***"cast me not away from thy presence and take not thy Holy Spirit away from me".*** So, the same scenario that played out with the first Adam in a garden, also played out with the last Adam, and in a garden as well. Whiles both involved a garden setting, both as well involved a tree, in that the sin of humanity committed by the first Adam, originated from the eating from a tree which Adam had been commanded by God not to eat from and the remedy for the sins of the first Adam and humanity in general, was paid on a tree, that's the wooden cross upon which Jesus the last Adam was hanged.

They lead Him to the cross which should be a wooden tree by the way because it was a tree that led to the fall of the first Adam and it was ordained that in like manner, it shall be upon a tree that the last Adam will redeem man.

From then, everything that happened afterwards was an exchange between the sinless lamb of God and sinful man.

The prophet Isaiah further captured this exchange so well in Isaiah 53 when he said.

> *He was wounded - for our transgression.*
> *He was bruised - for our iniquity.*
> *The chastisement of our peace - was upon Him.*
> *By His strips, - we are healed.*

My dear friend there cannot be a better exchange than this.

CHAPTER FIVE

INIQUITIES AND TRANSGRESSIONS

> ***5] But he was i) wounded for our transgressions, ii) he was bruised for our iniquities: iii) the chastisement of our peace was upon him; and iv) with his stripes we are healed.* Isaiah 53:5**

Isaiah, under the inspiration of God's Spirit, gives an amazingly accurate description of what happened when Jesus the Messiah was crucified.

The Prophet Isaiah captured the exchange that the death of Christ wrought for the fate of humankind in a more detailed manner when by the inspiration of the Spirit of God, he said,

He was wounded - *for our transgression.*
He was bruised - *for our iniquity.*
The chastisement of our peace - was upon Him.
By His strips -we are healed.

There cannot be a better exchange than this in that every pain and suffering that was inflicted upon Jesus, took care of a particular need in the lives of those He came to suffer and die for. Every action had a purpose, and every infliction had a goal to fulfill.

This passage of scripture is loaded with great insight, and it may take at least four to five teaching series to do justice to this text if I was to teach a bible study on this subject.

The suffering the Savior went through cannot be properly described as punishment because there cannot be punishment where there is no associated crime or offense.

It is especially so because both the bible and the judgement court of Pontius Pilate declared that no sin was found in Jesus. What Jesus did was that He took upon Himself the suffering which would secure the peace of those who had committed sin. This is contrary to the opinion of some bible Scholars and Theologians who claim that Christ's suffering was only a mental agony or an agony of the soul and not a physical torture leading to death. The word rendered "wounded" in this text means, to bore through, to perforate, to pierce. The word expresses a painful piercing and infliction of a physical nature done to different parts of the body.

(1) by the thorns in the head
(2) the nails in hands and feet

(3) by the spear of the soldier on side rib with the goal of puncturing the lungs

So, Christ suffering and crucifixion was not some mere mental agony of the soul. He was literally wounded and because the wounds alone is not enough to get the job done, he was also bruised in addition to the wounds.

It is my prayer that this powerful revelation that I am about to share will deepen your understanding of what Jesus accomplished on the cross of Calvary when He paid the ultimate price for the sins of humanity.

1) He was wounded for our transgressions.

The Hebrew word for *transgressions* can be translated *rebellion*, *trespass*, or *sin*. Transgressions here points to one's blatant, deliberate personal sin. Sin that clings to our lives and soul when we rebel against God's will, His plan, and His purpose for our lives. So, in brief my transgressions are my sins, my faults, and my shortcoming. They are not in relation to anybody or inherited from anyone. They are the results of my personal decisions, conducts, misconducts and actions in connection with no one else than myself.

The Message translation of the Bible puts it this way. *"Work hard for sin your whole life and your pension is death".* Now that Christ has atoned for our transgression through the wounds that he bore, let's look at the next marvelous thing our Lord Jesus Christ did for us.

2) He was bruised for our iniquities

While His wounds took care of your transgressions, something else was needed to take care of your iniquities and for that, He was bruised for your iniquities.

Iniquity has a way of putting its own twist on life, values, and mindsets because iniquity unlike our transgressions, does not usually originate from us but it's passed on to us.

What are iniquities

The meaning of the word "iniquity" comes from a Hebrew word that means *to twist, to distort or to bend.* Often an iniquity would start as a twisted version of the truth, or a slight distortion of the real thing. Getting even deeper into the meaning of the word, it seem like iniquity is different from transgression in that one's iniquity is related to something passed on to him or her whereas transgression is something you personally did. In other words, there is an element of cause and effect or some form of hereditary as far as iniquities are concern.

We read in **Deuteronomy 5:9-10** "***You shall not bow down to them or serve them; for I, the Lord your God, am a jealous God, visiting the iniquity of the fathers upon the children to the third and fourth generations of those who hate Me, and showing mercy and steadfast love to thousands and to a thousand generations of those who love Me and keep My commandments".***

What this text is teaching us is that the twisted and distorted things referred to as iniquities and some of which originated over three to four generations before us, can be transferred down to us through our genealogy and bloodlines. Do you know that your transgression committed today could become your children and grand-children's iniquity tomorrow? Well, that's why you must be careful how you live because you are not living for yourself only. We must tread our paths of faith carefully, doing so diligently with the generation that comes behind us in mind. Posterity would not forgive us if we failed to walk in ways that would leave godly impressions and footprints for our children and the generations behind us to walk therein.

Ephesians 5:15-16

> ***"15 See then that ye walk circumspectly, not as fools, but as wise,***
>
> ***16 Redeeming the time, because the days are evil.***

The above text admonishes the believer to walk circumspectly. Circumspect, is a term used in ocean navigation. The sail path is different from the path of the Pilot because the medium by which the vessel's flotation is possible is a liquid medium. Unlike travelling by air or by road where by one can simply follow a designated pathway. As a result of the variation of difference in the sail path, compared to the Pilot's pathway there is a way to set the sail path through the geographic positioning system GPS and other instruments and systems on the ship or vessel to aid navigation.

Circumspect means being careful to consider all circumstances and possible consequences. Circumspect is also used to describe the straitest sect in the New Testament era. The sect that is most precise and rigorous in their interpretation of the Mosaic law, and in observing even the more minute precepts of the law and tradition. Finally, to circumspect means to be diligent or to tread careful so as not to sway to the left or to the right.

Hence to be admonished by the word of God to walk "circumspectly" implies, the believer should ensure to navigate their spiritual pathway using spiritual instrument of navigation to aid their spiritual journey with the Lord. In other words, don't just navigate anyhow. One needs to navigate by the guidance of the Holy Spirit to know when to stop and when to go. When to sit and when to stand. When to engage and when to disengage. That is an example of a spiritual journey that's being aided by the spiritual navigation system which is the Holy Spirit. That's why it is troubling when you hear people say things like; *"I don't care what happens to the people around me after I am dead and gone from this earth"*. That's being careless, cruel, and selfish to say the least.

The bible says in Proverbs 13:22 ***"A good man leaveth an inheritance to his children's children".***

What this is telling us is that one should not only be thinking of themselves alone but also for the physical and spiritual wellbeing of their children and children's children. The point I want to emphasize here is that there are things you do today that can affect your children and their children into the third and fourth generations thereafter. Vice versa, things done by your parents and grandparents can immensely impart your life in a real way today. Notice how some behaviors like alcoholism, drug abuse, gambling and some peculiar health conditions, disease, and promiscuity, can run through the lives of people for generations in some families.

Why is that so? I believe it is because of iniquities in one's bloodline that has not been properly dealt with. Iniquity is a mystery the bible says. In Genesis 20 we read of Abraham and Sarah who journeyed to the South country. Abraham asked Sarah to tell Abimelech, the king of Gerar that she is Abraham's sister. This he did in fear that the king will kill him and take Sarah if Sarah was known to be his wife.

I have heard people say about this incident, that Abraham told a lie. That declaration by Abraham was not a lie, however it wasn't the full truth either because Sarah as a matter of fact was Abraham's half-sister who also became his wife at a later point in time. So, one will later come to find out that although this circumstance of twisting the truth was personal to Abraham, yet it later became an iniquity down his bloodline to the second, third and even fourth generations after him. This spirit of iniquity or as I may call it, twisting the truth became a bondage in the lives of the descendants of Abraham.

The king took Sarah into his chamber because he thought she was merely Abraham's sister because of what Abraham had told Sarah to tell the men of the land. However, in a dream the Lord exposed the whole truth to the king and the catastrophe that would have befall the king should he decide to touch Sarah although the king was ignorant of the full truth about the relationship between Abraham and Sarah. We ought to be careful about this because we know we are not supposed to lie as Christians so at times we don't lie but we also have a way of pushing the truth into a gray area to save our skin as some will put it. This is done in such a way that although it's not a liar, but neither is it the absolute truth, and that's what Abraham did.

He confessed the part of his relationship to Sarah that would save him from danger, but in so doing, he concealed the full truth by covering up part of the truth that he felt might hurt him. This is called "twisting the truth". And guess who is an expect and a master of twisting the truth? It is Satan. In Satan's first encounter with humanity (that's with Eve), he twisted the truth about the instructions that God had passed on to Eve through Adam.

He said to Eve in **Genesis 3:4–5.** ***4 And the serpent said unto the woman, Ye shall not surely die:***

> ***5 For God doth know that in the day ye eat thereof, then your eyes shall be opened, and ye shall be as gods, knowing good and evil.***

Genesis 3:1–5

> ***1 Now the serpent was more subtle than any beast of the field which the Lord God had made. And he said unto the woman, Yea, hath God said, Ye shall not eat of every tree of the garden?***
>
> ***2 And the woman said unto the serpent, we may eat of the fruit of the trees of the garden:***
>
> ***3 But of the fruit of the tree, which is in the midst of the garden, God hath said, Ye shall not eat of it, neither shall ye touch it, lest ye die.***
>
> ***4 And the serpent said unto the woman, Ye shall not surely die:***

> ***5 For God doth know that in the day ye eat thereof, then your eyes shall be opened, and ye shall be as gods, knowing good and evil.***

Notice the ability with which God created the serpent; *"it was subtle than any beast of the field which the Lord God had made".*

What does subtly mean? Most people will define it as being crafty or cunning, but more importantly to be subtle; means to have inner intention that is adequately maxed by ones' outwards actions. Notice that Creatures of the field, including human beings with such characters are very unpredictable because they have a way of making you feel very comfortable around them and then when you become comfortable and lose your guard, they pounce on you, and attack you at your most vulnerable point. Satan therefore knowing this, chose to appear as a serpent because of the degree of subtlety the serpent has. Notice that demon are persons except that they are persons without bodies hence they look for physical bodies to express themselves in. Notice that in the bible when Jesus addresses demons, he spoke to them as persons; just that they don't have bodies. So, demons can possess a dog, cats, pigs, as in the bible story in where the demon spirits pleaded with to cast them into the body of pigs. The question however is; why they usually choose to possess humans. It's because they look for creatures that they can have maximum expression through. So, the object is all about finding highest degree of expression. Therefore, Satan wanted to take advantage the highest degree of subtlety that is in the serpent compared to all creatures of the field that's why Satan chose he possess the serpent. This is because in the serpent he will have the most powerful expression of subtlety. Since Satan was up to the deception game he knows that if he wears the serpent and comes to Eve, he will be able to easily accomplish the deception he had in mind. That's his deception tactics. So, Satan came to Eve in the form of a serpent and said unto the woman, ***"Yea, hath God said, Ye shall not eat of every tree of the garden?***

Can you see that Satan's first appearance in the bible and to humanity is with questions? Satan came with questions because he has gaps in his knowledge database or information. Who told you that Satan knows the details of your life. That's not truth about the Satan bible reveals to us in the book of Genesis. Satan had to come and interact with questions before he was able to gain a full understanding to plant the seed of deception in the mind and heart of the woman. The traditions of men however, had made many to believe that Satan is all knowing like God. If you study your bible well, you know that cannot be the case because those attributes of God are what Satan wanted and coveted for that's why he was cast out of heaven. Note that the woman was the one who gave Satan all the information.

The woman said, verses 2-3

> ***2]And the woman said unto the serpent, we may eat of the fruit of the trees of the garden:***
>
> ***3 But of the fruit of the tree, which is in the midst of the garden, God hath said, Ye shall not eat of it, neither shall ye touch it, lest ye die.***

The woman gave away far too much, for the little question Satan asked and by the time she was done speaking, Satan now had a full understanding of what was happening.

Notice also that the original instructions was given to Adam alone and in fact, it was given to him before Eve was formed. So, God disciple only Adam. and it was Adam who later disciple Eve and passed on to Eve what God had instructed him about the tree. Adam told Eve that God said, "we should not touch it and we should not eat it." but notice that God did not tell Adam that they should not touch it. God only said they should not eat it.

Genesis 3:3

> ***"3 But of the fruit of the tree, which is in the midst of the garden, God hath said, Ye shall not eat of it, neither shall ye touch it, lest ye die.***

So, it means it was Adam who made his own additions to the original instructions that God had given. It was the man that told his wife Eve that God says we shouldn't touch it; so for instance if Eve was sweeping, dressing the garden or engaged in any activity in the garden and she happened to touch the tree and yet nothing happened, she will begin to have second thoughts about the instructions Adam passed on to her and begin to question the efficacy of all the other information that was passed on to her as well. Eve will say something like this to herself; "I was told God said we shouldn't touch it, and I touch it by accident or for whatever reason and nothing happened; so, if I am to eat it, most likely nothing will happen as well". It is therefore very likely that Eve was already opened to exploring before Satan came and told her *"You will not surely die."*

Satan therefore cashed in on the fact that a human being had altered the original instructions of God and added his own words to the instructions God had given. That is what we are seeing in the church circles today. Men by their own craftiness have altered the word of God in many ways. That thing that men have added to the word of God is going to be the same thing that's going to cause many to be deceived like Eve was and many to fall like both Adam and Eve were. There is so much going on in the church circles today that if you really study your bible and know the word of God, at times you have to stand back and say, "now wait a minute; so where did this come from and where did that gymnastics in church come from?"

I question myself almost every day about some of the things that we are seeing going on in church today. When you check the original manual of instructions from God (which is the Bible) most often, you don't find in the pages of scripture, what is being displayed in many churches today and one would wonder, if it's not in the original script then where are these things coming from. Just like in the case of Adam, if you take time and research into many of these things that goes on in churches today, you will find out that somebody at some point in time, decided to introduce their own thing into the original script that God had given. Today it said that we live in a dispensation of grace, however the kind of grace that is being preached from many pulpits across America and other parts of the world is not actually the kind of grace offered to us through the sacrifice Jesus paid with His own blood on the cross.

Through the ages there has been great men and women that rose up by the grace of God and as God began to use them, some started to drift away by adding their own take to the word of God and putting their own personal twist and preferences to many doctrines of the bible. No wonder today we have hundreds of Christian denominations some of which even have satanic roots but still call themselves Christians. May the Lord help us in our generations. In the next verse that follows, the Serpent responded to Eve and let's see what the serpent said, ***"Thou shall not surely die."***

In the Hebrew, this expression is the same as; *"in dying you shall surely die.* "Therefore, the idea in the Hebrew is that death is a process and not a onetime event. That means death is a continuous separation from God hence Adam became separated from God and began to function independent of God until he was totally cut off from God. However, in whatever state he ended up in; it was known as death. So, death is a process and the longer one stays in that state of separation from God it's death that's being manifested, because whatever state one lives in outside God, draws them in until it destroys them. That is how sin had always worked since it was introduced by man in the garden of Eden. Sin will always pull you in, until it blocks all avenues of getting of it, and then it ultimately destroys you. That is the technology of sin.

Notice that when Satan said, "thou shall not surely die' what Satan was saying to Eve was that she will be dead to the realm of God, but her eyes will be opened to other realms that are outside God. This notion and knowledge is what motivates people into witchcraft, occultism and to engage other powers of darkness because they seek for their eyes to be opened into other realms and by so doing, they become dead to the presence of the one true God of heaven. When people yield themselves to Satan, they are not able to know the realm of God, but they get to know another realm that eventually alienate them from God.

Look at the verse 5 and you will see the product that Satan is selling to many todays. What they were not aware is that they were already God because they were created in the image of God, and hence there was no need for them to be offered the promise of being like God, which is a position and authority they already had. Today, Satan's merchandise has not changed. He is still selling everything possible to man to rob men of their soul which is far more precious than what he is selling to them. Note that while the woman was genuinely deceived, Adam on the other hand chose to willingly rebel against God's command because Satan knew that he couldn't deceive Adam and that's why he targeted the woman. So, in effect, two sins were committed in Eden. The woman's sin was buying into deception and Adam's sin was rebelling against the commandment God had given him.

Now this first error of offering a partial truth had to do with Abraham, but let's move on to the next generation after Abraham to see what happened next. In Genesis 26 we read that Isaac and Rebekah, who are Abraham's son, and daughter in law journey down to Gerar because of a famine in the land. Does the name of the place ring a bell in your mind about Abraham? When they arrived in Gerar some of the men asked Isaac about Rebekah and he told them that she was his sister! Again, Abimelech the king saw that she was his wife and had to expose the lie for what it was. Isn't that interesting.

Read; **Genesis 26:1-11.**
It is interesting to note the following.

The same place - (Gerar)
The same king - (Abimelech)
The same circumstance - (Twisting the truth about their wives in fear for their lives)

Years before, Abraham told a twisted version of the truth in Gerar and now when faced with a similar situation his son Isaac also reverted to a lie. Only this time with Isaac, it was not half-truth and half lie but rather a blatant lie. If you lower your standard of holiness today, the next generation after you will do less or go even lower than you did. That's why we must always keep the highest standards there is so that should the generations after us fall below our standards, they wouldn't fall so low and so bad.

While good heritage has the propensity to get better down the line, bad heritage on the other hand, gets bad and even worse down the generational line. Abraham's twist got twisted even further by his son Isaac. What's happening here is that "Abraham's transgression became Isaac's iniquity" because a seed of deception was sown down the bloodline through Abraham's conduct. So whiles transgression is on a personal level, iniquity on the hand is a by-product which is passed down ones' bloodline from one generation to another.

Abraham may think his back is against the wall, so he twisted the truth to get him off the hook, but that twisted truth years later became even more twisted down his bloodline through his son Isaac.

With some people.

1) the reason why their children are not serious with the Lord and shows no interest or commitment to the things of God is because they lack commitment themselves.
2) the reason why some of your family members or your spouse or children don't want to give their lives to Christ nor have anything to do with the church is because they hear you gossip about other church brethren at home.

I believe your family members who are not saved may be saying to themselves, "if this is what goes on in church, then they don't want any part of the mess you gossip about in their presence". I used to know an unsaved husband of one church sister several years ago. This gentleman knew so much about the church than most members who attended that church knew and yet this man had never been to that church. So how did he know so much about the church and what goes on within and yet has never been to the church or attended any service or church meeting? Is it through dreams and visions from the Lord? No, I don't think so. It is through the gossip he has been hearing his wife engage in over the phone with other members of that church.

Abraham was only a first generation "half-liar." His Son Isaac became second generation "complete liar." But are you ready to investigate what the third generation after Abraham was like? Isaac and his wife Rebekah had twin sons called Jacob and Esau. The name Jacob means "heel-catcher, supplanter or deceiver". According to the bible accounts, Jacob deceived his father as well as lied about his identity by twisting the truth to obtain the special blessing and favor that was supposed to go to his brother Esau who was the first born. But Jacob was only the third generation from Abraham. Four generations from Abraham, Simeon, and Levi through deception, circumcised the men of Shechem and on the third day when the men were sour, they slew them all. Gen 34:25-30

Can't you see a clear pattern or trend playing out through the direct descendants of Abraham? What originated from Abraham as a half-truth and half-lie grows through the generations of Abraham. It is passed on to Isaac his son who told a blatant lie and now to Jacob his grandson; whose character became twisted and ended up with a deceptive personality and now to Abraham's great grand-children Simeon and Levi who slaughtered the men of Shechem through deception. What's happening here is that Abraham opened a door to satanic invasion through his transgression and his son, grandson, and great grandsons stepped in through that door of iniquity generations after. Iniquities are real and create real challenges in the lives of so many Christians. Iniquities give the enemy legal grounds to attack and deceive generations of people through the transgressions on their ancestors. Iniquity is a mystery based on spiritual equity and justice. But the good news about what makes the finished work of Jesus Christ on the cross so powerful is that not only did He dealt decisively with our transgressions, but also He paved the way for our iniquities to be dealt with.

5) he was wounded for our transgressions, (but the story did not end there) because he was also bruised for our iniquities:

His wounds alone couldn't do it all so, God would have it that Christ Jesus will also be bruised in addition to the wounds to take care of our iniquities. Regardless of what iniquities you have been exposed to through your bloodline, in the name of Jesus they will all be neutralized by the blood of sprinkling that speaks better things than the blood of Abel. Christ was bruised on the cross. The word used here (אכד dâkâ') properly means to be broken into pieces, every piece covers members of your bloodline down the generations to come.

Difference between Wounds and Bruises

I pulled this information on the difference between wounds and bruises from an article of medicine written and reviewed by a renowned medical practitioner by name Dr. Ajay Kumar Pujala

According to this medical expert, wounds and bruises are both injuries, however they differ widely in terms of the following.

1) the causing factors,
2) the nature of the injury,
3) the pain they cause and
4) the kind of treatment they require.

(Written and reviewed by Dr. Ajay Kumar Pujala, FHM Fellowship in HIV Medicine, MD, MBBS. HIV Specialist, Hyderabad • 22years experience.)

What drew my attention the most is the fourth point he made about the difference between wounds and bruises. He stated that wounds differ from bruises based on the kind of treatment they require. I found that to be profound in relation to what Christ died on the cross to accomplish our salvation according to Isaiah's prophecy.

According to the article by this medical expert,

1) A wound is usually caused by a sharp object, but bruises are the results of blunt force or trauma.
2) Whiles wounds causes quick damage with skin tissue cut or punctured, a bruise is where the skin is not torn

3) Wound almost certainly bleeds due to ruptured tissue and blood vessels. Bruises causes blood to accumulate under the skin tissue, creating dark patch of skin.

Some of us were born with dark patches of iniquity through our bloodline, but the good news is that Jesus dealt with those dark patches of iniquities as well. Oh Hallelujah, just thinking about this makes me feel like jumping and shouting.

The Mystery of Iniquity

II Thessalonians 2:7

> ***7 For the mystery of iniquity doth already work: only he who now letteth will let, until he be taken out of the way.***

Notice the bible did not say transgressions are a mystery, but it says iniquities are. The mystery about your iniquities are that, although they originated in your bloodline before you were born, yet still you are guilty of them through blood association with the people who committed the actual act that brought about the iniquity. This is because although you were not physically present at the time, yet you were present through the loins of them that committed the act generations before you were born. One may ask what is meant by that? Let me explain further.

Hebrews 7:9-10 says.

> ***9] And as I may so say, † Levi also, who receiveth tithes, payed tithes in Abraham.***

10] For he was yet in the loins of his father, when Melchisedec met him.

This is what makes iniquity a mystery. Although Levi was not present in person when Abraham met Melchizedek on his way home from the battlefield, but Levi is said to have paid tithes to Melchizedek through the loins of Abraham, who by the way lived hundreds of years before his descendent Levi was born.

Besides, it is interesting to note that in Psalm 94:20 iniquity is portrayed as having its own throne. The bible never mentioned at any point that sins or transgressions have thrones, but it says in Psalm 94 that iniquity has a throne. What this is teaching us about iniquity is that iniquities are established through generations and usually have a long reign from one generation to the other until it's dealt with in a proper manner. The reason why iniquity has a throne is because it can reign through several generations within a family or bloodline. A throne also suggest that iniquity has a kingdom over which it reigns because thrones and reigns are always associated with rulership over kingdoms.

Psalm 94:20-21 say,

20 Shall the throne of iniquity have fellowship with thee, which frameth mischief by a law?

21 They gather themselves together against the soul of the righteous and condemn the innocent blood.

There are two things that are worthy to notice through the above scripture.

1. Iniquities committed through the shedding of innocent blood is a mystery.
2. Iniquity itself is portrayed as having a throne. If iniquity has a throne, then it has a reign, and that explains why iniquities can run from generation to generations within a family or ones' bloodline.

Furthermore, we read in Psalm 32:5

> ***"I acknowledged my sin to You and my iniquity Have I not hid'.***

The writer of this psalm can't hide his iniquity because it could be found by tracing it down his bloodline hence how can it be hidden. The writer goes on to say that,

> ***I said, I will confess my transgressions to the Lord, and thou forgave the iniquity of my sin.***

1 John 1:8-9 says.

> ***"If we say we have no sin, we deceive ourselves, and the Truth is not in us. If we [freely] admit that we have sinned and confess our sins, He is faithful and just and will forgive our sins (transgressions) and cleanse us from all unrighteousness (iniquity)***

Transgressions are forgiven, iniquities are cleansed

While sin and transgression are forgiven, iniquities are cleansed because sin or transgression are on a personal level. However, iniquities run deep in bloodline through generations, hence they need cleansing.

The word "cleanse" speaks of purification in a levitical sense. In the Old Testament, the role of the High Priest was two-fold.

1) The Priest and Levites in bible times took care of all the sacrifices for sin (transgressions) in the temple, but that was not their only role.

If someone was unclean due to leprosy or some sort of disease, they went to the priests as well and after they've gone through a whole list of rituals, they are declared as being clean only by the Priest. In like manner, Jesus being our High Priest also did the same for us when He Himself became the Sacrifice. And it was His blood that cleansed us.

Psalm 65:3

Iniquities prevail against me: as for our transgressions, thou shalt purge them away.

The victory report is that "the evil cycles that unhindered iniquity can establish in your life and in the lives of your family are broken because of what Jesus did on the cross."

3. With His Stripes we are healed.

Healing is an integral part of Christ's atonement on the cross. We should not be begging and screaming hopelessly for our healing because according to Jesus, healing ought to be the children's bread. Not only can we get forgiveness for our sins and cleansing for our iniquities. We can also receive health and healing based on the finished work of redemption that Christ Jesus accomplished on the cross of Calvary on our behalf. The lack of faith, coupled with unbelief has robbed many born-again believers of their healing, which is supposed to be the most common blessing of the believer. If you can believe in Christ for eternal salvation, it implies you have enough faith to also believe in Him for healing which I would say is temporal because it meant only for this earth. I use the word "temporal" because according to the bible, your healing pertains to this earth only. Since there are no sicknesses and diseases in heaven, healing will not be needed in heaven. Salvation is eternal life guaranteed, but healing is only for this earth. God has not changed that's why we still see so many miracles of salvation and of healing in His house every time we gather to worship Him. His love for us has not changed. He longs to see us saved as well as healed because healing is indeed the children's bread.

Isaiah 53 says by his strips ye are healed. According to ancient Roman law, after an offender has been given forty strips, they were supposed to be set free. So, giving someone forty minus one strip which equals thirty-nine, means the offender is still not to be freed. Hence, they gave Jesus thirty-nine stripes so that they will go on and be permitted by the law to crucify Him instead of setting Him free. The reason why his strips could heal us is because he did not attach any offense to the thirty-nine strips he was beaten.

Offense is the number one killer of spiritual strength, anointing and spiritual power of the believer. But because Jesus died to forgive all, including even those who unjustly and without cause crucified Him death could not hold Him down in His grave in that He rose again on the third day. Many people have laid down their life, shed their blood, and gone the extra mile for the sake of their faith in God, but what's holding their victory is the spirit of unforgiveness which often leads to offense. John the Baptist toward the end of his life, took offense to the fact that Jesus did not come to his rescue when he was thrown into prison. Many are those who have taken God's business too personal and into their own hands, and as a result, they are hurt because of what people has said about them. They have become bitter because of what people has done to them. They are angry because of how people have treated them, or resentful because of the perception others have about them.

Hebrews 12:15

> ***Looking diligently lest any man fail of the grace of God; lest any root of bitterness springing up trouble you, and thereby many be defiled.***

This phrase *"Any root of bitterness"* is very interesting. It did not say "lest any bitterness trouble you". It says, lest any *root of bitterness* because bitterness by its' nature, can develop roots in the life of its victims. The apostle here alludes to Deuteronomy 29:18. In that chapter Moses had again brought before the people the covenant which, nearly forty years before, had been made and ratified in Horeb, the mount of God. (See Hebrews 9:18-20).

Deuteronomy 29:18, ***Lest there should be among you man, or woman, or family, or tribe, whose heart turneth away from the Lord, lest there should be a root that beareth gall and wormwood.***

It is clear that Deuteronomy 29:18, was on the writer's mind when he was writing to warn the Jewish believers in Hebrews 12.

> ***Lest there should be among you a root that beareth gall and wormwood.***

That's a poisonous herb. That which springs from the root is not merely bitter, but it is also poisonous.

The hidden truth in this saying is that,

1) Those who orchestrate *"root of bitterness"* within any church, are themselves the first victims of their action. The root of bitterness usually troubles those who orchestrate it before it catches on to others.
2) Because bitterness has a root, so long as it is hidden under the earth it cannot be remedied, but when it "springs up" there is the need for it to be dealt with immediately and boldly otherwise it will spread on to other members of the body.
3) The spirit of bitterness could be present in one's life and nobody may know it until the root gradually reveals its pernicious character by springing up.

That's why the bible says mark those who curse division and strife among the brethren. If there are not marked deliberately, their presence in the body may not be identified.

In Acts 8:23 the Apostle Peter referred to the same chapter in Deuteronomy as he spoke to Simon Magus, who above all other men, proved to be a root of bitter poison in the early Church. While the word of God says vengeance belong to God, many have taken vengeance into their own hands and their actions have rather hurt people instead of healing the wound inflicted on them.

In verse 5; every pain and suffering Jesus went through was meant to take care of a need in the life of the believer.

1. *His wounds - took care of our transgressions.*
2. *His bruises - took care of our iniquities.*
3. *His chastisement- took care of our peace.*
4. *His stripes - took care of our healing.*

The difference between sin, transgression and iniquity is that when one is guilty of shedding blood, it's beyond sin or transgression. It becomes iniquity which travels down the bloodline of the person who shed the blood until that iniquity is cleansed. Also notice that while sins are pardoned, iniquities on the other hand must be cleansed because it can be passed on from one generation to the other.

Moreover, the bible declares that in His death, Jesus went down to hell and hades. This was necessary because since the fate of the sinner was bound to hell, that's why Jesus had to descend to hell according to **Revelation 1:18.**

> ***I am he that liveth, and was dead; and behold, I am alive for evermore, Amen; and have the keys of hell and of death.***

He said I have the keys to hell and death meaning Jesus collected the keys from Satan in hell after he rose from the death. Otherwise, where would He have gotten the keys to the kingdom that he later entrusted into the hands of Peter and the other disciples from? In addition to that, Isaiah 61 says Jesus opened the prison doors to all the captives after he collected the keys. For if the princes of this world had known the magnitude of the victory Christ's death will win for the sinner, they wouldn't have crucified the king of glory. That's why every time the blood is mentioned it reminds Satan not only of his ignorance of God's plan of salvation, but also of his total defeat and the ultimate doom that awaits him and his subjects. It is worth noting that when the true born-again believer pleads the blood of Jesus against Satan and against the works of darkness, it is really calling out the price and proof of the believer's redemption from sin, shame, and condemnation that's why Satan can't stand it.

CHAPTER SIX

INIQUITY OF THE AMORITES

The Iniquity of the Amorites

In Genesis 15, God confirms His unconditional covenant with Abraham. God promises Abraham a multitude of descendants who will inherit the land in which Abraham sojourns. God then apprehended Abraham with a brief timeline of future events in the verse 13 by saying to him.

> ***"Know for certain that for four hundred years your descendants will be strangers in a country not their own and that they will be enslaved and mistreated there".*** (Genesis 15:13).

God told him of the captivity that was to come upon his descendant in the future and how that they were going to be carried into captivity in a strange land for 400 years. That was indeed not a happy news for Abraham hence he was troubled that this was going to happen to his descendants. God therefore began to unveil to him in another statement more details of what was to befall his descendants and the reason for it, in the verse 16.

> ***"And then, In the fourth generation your descendants will come back here, for the sin of the Amorites has not yet reached its full measure". (Verse 16).***

The Timeline

The return of Abraham's descendants from the strange land, would coincide with God's judgment on the Amorites who dwell in the land of Canaan. These prophecies were fulfilled when after Joseph's death, Pharaoh enslaved the Israelites who were living in Egypt at the time, and then, four hundred years after Joseph, Moses brought the children of Israel out of Egypt to the borders of Canaan. Joshua then led the people into Canaan and conquered the land. Joshua's conquest took place only after the sin of the Canaanites had "reached its full measure" (Genesis 15:16).

The Reason

The reason for these 400 years of captivity in Egypt is because the land that God had promise to Abraham's descendants was still in custody of people the Amorites. The Amorites had entitlement to that land in that they were the first settlers, so God being a just God, did not want to take the land out of the hands of its first settlers without a just cause although God owns the land and He had promised to give it unto Abraham and his descendants. However, it shall come to pass when the iniquity of the Amorites fills the cup, then God will act because then they will forfeit the right to the land by virtue of the fullness of their iniquity that had come before the Lord. This follows a similar principle in the case of the destruction of Sodom and Gomorrah. The bible says the wickedness of their sins came before the Lord and the Lord Himself came down with two ranking angels to see what was going on in Sodom.

Genesis 15:16

> ***16 But in the fourth generation they shall come hither again: for the iniquity of the Amorites is not yet full.***

Genesis 15:16 seem to suggest that there is a cup by which God measures the volume of men's evil doing and iniquity upon the surface of the earth, and that God's judgement comes down upon humanity only when that cup of iniquity is full.

It is interesting to note that the text above seem to suggest that there is a cup by which God measures the volume of men's evil doing and iniquity upon the surface of the earth. So, God told Abraham that the reason why the land of the Amorites cannot be transferred immediately into the hands of his descendants, and because of which they had sojourn in a strange land for 400 years is because the cup that measures the iniquity of the Amorites is not yet full and hence there is no just cause to turn over the land upon which they dwell to the descendants of Abraham. That means it's going to take some time for the fullness of the iniquity of the Amorites to be achieved. Hence the residency of Abraham's descendants in Egypt was a waiting period, or a stop-gap measure implemented by God to fill in the time span until the iniquity of the Amorite is full. The same analogy is alluded to in Revelations chapter 18 where the great city of Babylon is described with its ultimate destruction.

> ***18 And after these things I saw another angel come down from heaven, having great power; and the earth was lightened with his glory.***
>
> ***[2] And he cried mightily with a strong voice, saying, Babylon the great is fallen, is fallen, and is become the habitation of devils, and the hold of every foul spirit, and a cage of every unclean and hateful bird.***
>
> ***[3] For all nations have drunk of the wine of the wrath of her fornication, and the kings of the earth have committed fornication with her, and the merchants of the earth are waxed rich through the abundance of her delicacies.***
>
> ***[4] And I heard another voice from heaven, saying, Come out of her, my people, that ye be not partakers of her sins, and that ye receive not of her plagues.***
>
> ***[5] For her sins have reached unto heaven, and God hath remembered her iniquities.***
>
> ***[6] Reward her even as she rewarded you, and double unto her double according to her works: in the cup which she hath filled fill to her double.***

Notice that the sixth verse makes mention of the filling of the cup of Babylon's iniquity. Finally, I would like you to notice two things about the Babylon referred to in the above passage.

1) It is different from the city of Babylon described in the book of Daniel where Daniel, Meshach, Shadrach, Abednego, and the Jews were taken into captivity for 70 years. The description in Revelations 18 is three-dimensional in that it is viewed and described through the eye of the mighty Angel from the realm of the Spirit, while the physical city of Babylon is two-dimensional.
2) While the physical city of Babylon described in the book of Daniel is a governance over a city, region, or territory regardless of its expanse, the Babylon referred to in the book of Revelations chapter 18 appears to have developed into a worldwide system under whose umbrella the governance of all nations fall. This is noted clearly in the third verse of Revelations 18.

While in the book of Daniel, we see Babylon the "place". In the book of Revelation however, we see Babylon the "system".

3 For all nations have drunk of the wine of the wrath of her fornication, and the kings of the earth have committed fornication with her, and the merchants of the earth are waxed rich through the abundance of her delicacies.

Nature of The Iniquities of the Amorites

During the time of Moses, God gave the reason for the Canaanites' downfall:

> ***The land was defiled; so, I punished it for its sin, and the land vomited out its inhabitants. (Leviticus 18:25).***

The entire context of Leviticus 18 and Leviticus 20 captures in detail what the inhabitants of the land were doing prior to God "vomiting them out of the land" and the taking over of the land by Israel, under the able leadership of Joshua. The sins of the Amorites includes,

- *Uncovering the nakedness of mom, dad, sister, brother, aunt, uncle etc.*
- *Offering children to god Molech. (i.e., burn babies - type of ancient abortion deemed necessary with unwanted children created by the behaviors listed in these chapters.)*
- *Not lie with a male as with a woman.*
- *Not mate with an animal.*
- *Turn to mediums and familiar spirits.*
- *Cursing father or mother.*
- *Commit adultery with neighbor's wife.*
- *Lies with fathers' wife.*
- *Lies with daughter in law.*
- *Man lies with man.*
- *Marry mom and daughter.*
- *Lies with sister.*
- *Lies with woman when she has a flow of blood.*
- *Taking brothers wife.*

- *The land (of Canaan/Amorite) is defiled... all these abominations the men of the land have done, who were before you, and thus the land(Canaan/Amorite) is defiled.*
- *You shall not walk in the statues of the nation(Canaan/ Amorite) which I am casting out from before you; for they commit all these things, and therefore I abhor them.*

The role of the land in this case is to serve as the accountant in that, it is the land that will bear the record and when the cup of iniquity of the Amorites is full.

The role of the land in this case is to serve as the accountant in that it is the land that will bear the record and when that cup of iniquity of the Amorites is full. They will no longer have rights to the land, and the land will help Israel in that it will cry out and announce to the universal court of heaven for justice against the Amorites.

So, the implication here is that it will take 400 years for the iniquity of the Amorites to reach the tipping point of the cup that measures iniquity of the Amorites. This means the 400 years of captivity of the children of Israel in Egypt is not because they did sin against the Lord but rather it was a stop-gap measure to wait while the fullness of the iniquity of the Amorite is reached. Notice therefore that unlike Israel's 70 years of captivity in Babylon which was a punishment because of their sin, their captivity in Egypt on the other hand was not provoked by sin. This is just like the babe Jesus was taken into hiding in Egypt to keep Him from the fury of King Harold until Harold was dead. That means after the 400 years when the fullness of the iniquity of the Amorites is reached, the land that keeps records will help Israel by crying out on their behalf for justice to be done.

As an example, Lot the nephew of Abraham was not saved from the judgment upon Sodom because of the result of Abraham's negotiation with God. While Abraham stopped at 10 people during his negotiations with God about sparing Sodom, it still fell short because Lot's household was made up of a total of 8 people. That includes Lot, his wife, their two unmarried daughters, their two married daughters and their husbands.

Notice that when the iniquity of Sodom reached the attention of God and God came down Himself with two ranking Angels to see, although Abrahams' negotiation with God for mercy, stopped at ten people but the life of Lot and his household was still spared despite. This is besides those members of his family who were either not willing to come along with Lot and his wife who failed to obey the simple instructions of the Angels and hence turned into a statue of salt. It means that God overlooked the outcome of that negotiation with Abraham and still showed mercy to Lot because of the closeness of the relationship God had with Abraham. With God there is abundant of mercy and His mercy results in redemption. That's why Lot was saved even though Abraham's negotiation with God could not yield the kind of result that could save Lot.

Lessons Learnt

The conquest of Canaan served the dual purpose of punishing the Amorites for their sin and giving the Israelites a land of their own. One thing Genesis 15:16 shows is the certainty of God's judgment on the wicked. The Amorites and other Canaanites nations were exceedingly wicked (for a list of some of their sins, see Leviticus 18). At the same time, Genesis 15:16 demonstrates God's love, mercy, and above all His longsuffering and patience with sinful man. Rather than immediately wipe out the Amorites, God chose to wait for over four hundred years to bring judgment upon them.

They were given ample time to turn from their wickedness, turn to God, and be forgiven. The Amorites had a chance to repent and be saved from the wrath and judgement of God, just like the Assyrians in Nineveh did during in the time of the Prophet Jonah. The Amorites' sin had not escaped God's notice. He was keeping track of the measure of their sins, and during Abraham's time, it was not yet full. So, the Amorites were warned that judgment was coming but it is sad that they did not take advantage of their time of grace.

They wasted their four hundred years and continued to fill up the measure of their iniquity. Because the Amorites finally filled up the measure of their sin, God brought Joshua and the children of Israel against them. God's command was for the Israelites to "completely destroy them—the Hittites, Amorites, Canaanites, Perizzites, Hivites and Jebusites—as the Lord your God has commanded you" (Deuteronomy 20:17). The Amorites fought back, but God destroyed them before Israel and gave them the Amorites' land (Joshua 24:8).

It is commonly said that history always repeats itself. It is worth noting that in today's civilization, most modern countries have started to fully embrace, teach, and are entertained with all forms of Canaanite and Amorite behavior and lifestyle. It is worth mentioning that majority of movies, TV shows, and Internet-shows you see contain forms of Amorite behavior. This gives a dangerous signal of where our present-day civilization is heading toward. If the iniquities of the Amorites were measure in God's cup of judgement, then you can bet that the measurement of the iniquities of our present-day civilization is already under way. While God is patience and long-suffering, his patience will not last forever because there is another nature in God called the justice of God.

The Full Cup of the Guilty

God is a *just* God, who will by no means clear the guilty (Exodus 34:7). There can come a time when someone's cup is full. There can come a time when God's mercy no longer extends to them, and where God in His perfect wisdom sees that all His mercy bestowed upon them will never be accepted. The time can come, when they're *past* redemption, when they have sinned away their opportunity. John Bunyan relates a vignette in *The Pilgrim's Progress* about a man in the iron cage as someone who had sinned away his opportunity and could no longer repent. For no one can repent unless God gives them repentance, because repentance is a gift of God. Only God can give repentance. We can tell that person to ask God to give them repentance, but God alone grants repentance. We don't often hear about God *granting* repentance, and yet this is clearly taught in the New Testament:

> *"Him God has exalted to His right hand to be Prince and Savior,* **to give repentance to Israel** *and forgiveness of sins."*

Acts 5:31

> *When they heard these things they became silent; and they glorified God, saying, "Then* **God has also granted to the Gentiles repentance** *to life."*

Acts 11:18

> *...in humility correcting those who are in opposition,* **if God perhaps will grant them repentance**, *so that they may know the truth...*

2 Timothy 2:25

> As an example, In Acts 12, we find that God no longer has repentance for King Agrippa; the Lord waited until his cup was full. And very soon the last drop was put into his cup.

> *Now Herod had been very angry with the people of Tyre and Sidon; but they came to him with one accord and having made Blastus the king's personal aide their friend, they asked for peace, because their country was supplied with food by the king's country.* *Acts 12:20*

Herod was angry with the people of Tyre and Sidon. But at last, through Blastus, Herod's aide and confidant (who apparently received a bribe), Herod was made willing to make friends with the people of Tyre and Sidon again. Just before we proceed, let me ask you a question: Did you notice in the narrative in Acts 12 that the angel sent from God to set Peter free was a great delivering angel, and that he was a *smiting* or *striking* angel? He struck Peter on the side and said, "Get up!" (Acts 12:7). That's important to keep in mind as the narrative in Acts 12 continues, because apparently the angel didn't immediately return to heaven, since he hadn't yet finished his assignment. He was still around, waiting....

Strike or smite is the English translation of the Greek verb *patássō* (πατάσσω). In the New Testament it appears a total of ten times, eight occurrences of which are outside of this chapter. We hear *patássō* in Jesus' quotation of Zechariah 13:7 (in Matthew 26:31 || Mark 14:27); and it describes the attack of the disciples on the servant of the high priest in the Garden of Gethsemane (Matthew 26:31 || Luke 22:49 and 50). *Patássō* is also used of Moses striking the Egyptian (Acts 7:24), of the two prophets *striking* the earth (Revelation 11:6), and of the triumphant, returning Lord Jesus *striking down* the nations (Revelation 19:15). That accounts for the eight times *patássō* appears outside of Acts 12, the chapter we have under consideration. We will count the sharp, hasty awakening of Peter in Acts 12:7 as the ninth appearance of the verb. And, as we shall soon see in the text, we are about to encounter the tenth and final appearance in the climax of this chapter.

> *So on a set day Herod, arrayed in royal apparel, sat on his throne and gave an oration to them.*
> *Acts 12:21*

Josephus, the Jewish historian, records that Herod went into the great amphitheater, dressed in a garment of silver. And he spoke to the gathered throng as the sun rose in the morning, just as the first rays of the sun came beaming into the amphitheater. (He wouldn't have spoken later because of the heat of the day.) Those beams of sunlight shone on Herod as he stood on that great forum before the people. The sunlight reflected and dazzled off the silver fabric, shining back with a radiance as if he himself were a god.

Here is Flavius Josephus' account of the incident (in his *Antiquities of the Jews,* XIX.8.2):

> *...he {Agrippa} put on a garment made wholly of silver, and of a contexture truly wonderful, and came into the theater early in the morning; at which time the silver of his garment being illuminated by the fresh reflection of the sun's rays upon it, shone out after a surprising manner, and was so resplendent as to spread a horror over those that looked intently upon him.*

Combine Herod Agrippa's gifted oratory, his shining, god-like appearance, and the crowd's purpose of flattering their benefactor, and the stage is now set for God's judgment.

> *And the people kept shouting, "The voice of a god and not of a man!"* Acts 12:22

Their flattery was elevated to praise which should only be offered to God; and Herod accepted it! Immediately his cup was full, and the smiting angel was still around:

> *Then immediately an angel of the Lord* struck *him because he did not give glory to God. And he was eaten by worms and died.* Acts 12:23

It is quite one thing to be "smitten" by an angel to rouse you up and deliver you, as happened with Peter in the prison cell. It's another thing, if you're intentionally wicked and resist God, for that smiting angel to put you to death. Such are God's counteractions that He has reserved a special and awful end for great persecutors of the saints.[42] Normally, people die, are buried, and then are "eaten by worms." But Herod Agrippa I was eaten by worms even while he was alive.

Percy Gutteridge noted as an aside that "Herod the Great {grandfather of Agrippa I} died of an awful disease… his body was in such a corrupt and putrid condition in his living death that even his attendants fled. They couldn't be with him." Here is Josephus' account:

> *But now Herod's distemper greatly increased upon him after a severe manner, and this by God's judgment upon him for his sins; for a fire glowed in him slowly, which did not so much appear to the touch outwardly, as it augmented his pains inwardly; for it brought upon him a vehement appetite to eating, which he could not avoid to supply with one sort of food or other. His entrails were also ex-ulcerated, and the chief violence of his pain lay on his colon; an aqueous and transparent liquor also had settled itself about his feet, and a like matter afflicted him at the bottom of his belly. Nay, further, his privy-member was putrefied, and produced worms; and when he sat upright, he had a difficulty of breathing, which was very loathsome, on account of the stench of his breath, and the quickness of its returns; he had also convulsions in all parts of his body, which increased his strength to an insufferable degree. It was said by those who pretended to divine, and*

> *who were endued with wisdom to foretell such things, that God inflicted this punishment on the king on account of his great impiety…*
>
> *o Antiquities XVII.6.5*

In considering Herod Agrippa's horrible death, let's not lose sight of how God's victory ended up:

> [24]*But the word of God grew and multiplied.* [25]*And Barnabas and Saul returned from Jerusalem when they had fulfilled their ministry, and they also took with them John whose surname was Mark.* (Acts 12:24-25)

CHAPTER SEVEN

MYSTERIES IN BLOOD

I mentioned in the previous chapters of this book that everything about blood is mystical. In this chapter, I will expound on this statement by citing a few examples from different functions of blood.

1) Blood Pre-dates the foundations of the World.

The bible refers to Jesus as the lamb that was slain from the foundation of the world. Meaning that long before there was an Adam and Eve upon the earthly realm of existence, blood was shed. Therefore, blood is not just something the existence of which originated with creation of the beast of the earth or man. Blood existed before the foundations of the world. How and in what manner or container or vessel it existed in, no one knows.

2) Blood has custody and is custodian of all that is ancestral.

Blood has custody and is the custodian of everything ancestral, that is why the blood of our ancestors still runs through our veins.

Blood is the custody and the custodian of everything ancestral. Everything ancestral as used here, means blood is what keeps track of our ancestry through generations. Every dealing of man is recorded in blood, and these includes the records of all our activities here on earth. All your earthly activities are recorded and stored in blood.

As an example, a few years ago my wife was diagnosed with a medical condition that affected her muscle strength. At the peak of her health crises, it was so bad that she couldn't even brush her teeth by herself or swallow her own saliva because her muscles did not have the needed energy to hold the brush, much more to swing it back and forth or coordinate any activity of the body that employs the use of muscle strength. At times, she felt like she was choking on her own saliva. In the process of time and with much prayer, fasting and the support of family, friends, the church, and the prayer of saints around the world, this disease that Doctors told her there is no cure for, has almost gone into remission. As a result, she was told by her team of doctors not to engage in activities that would strain her muscles. She was also supposed to go in for a periodic medical check-up which includes regular blood test with her team of doctors.

Upon realizing that she would need some basic exercise periodically just to keep her fit and healthy, she decided to go on the treadmill and to engage in a few routine exercises at home. Just around that time when she started to exercise against the advice of her doctors, she was due her next medical check-up. During that check-up, they took her blood samples to the lab for examination. When the result came back, she was surprised to get a call from her doctor, asking her about what kind of hectic work or tasks she has been engaging in. She was surprised how the doctors got to know that she has been excising, because she never mentioned it to them. But her doctor made her aware that the results of her blood work shows that she has been doing some form of rigorous physical tasks or exercise. She then admitted to her doctors that she has been trying to exercise to keep healthy and physically fit. When she came home and shared this experience with me, I looked at her and said, "well, don't blame anyone about the fact that your doctors had gotten to know that you have been exercising. Your own blood has betrayed you, told on you as well as revealed your secret workouts to your doctors". It was very surprising to her and to me as well to know that every rigorous activity that she was engaged in was being recorded in her blood. Could you imagine that?

3) Blood Keeps Record

Luke 22:20. Likewise ***also the cup after supper, saying, this cup is the New Testament in my blood which is shed for you.***

In the above text, Jesus speaks about the New Testament in His blood. There are two key points and questions that needs to be answered from this scripture to fully understand it.

A) What is a Testament?

A testament is a legal document that keeps records of vital legal matters or information that needs to be implemented upon the death of a person. And so, if a testament is a vital record, then according to the above text in Luke 22;20, where are these records stored or kept? Jesus then tells us that the New Testament or records or legal information and documents are kept or stored in His blood. I could take another whole chapter to expound deeper into this subject however, the key point to note is simply this, records are stored in blood.

The reason why although Jesus died over 2000 years ago and yet salvation is still potent and transferable through the name of Jesus is because of the records of His atonement that are stored in his blood.

---

i) Every record of what Christ suffered and came to do for the redemption of the sins of humanity are stored in His blood.

ii) While no records stored in His blood can be erased because they are eternal records, yet Jesus' blood can erase, blot-out or over-ride other handwriting of ordinances that have been written against the sinner for whom Christ died on the cross to save. That explains why the bible says that the blood of Jesus speaks better things than the blood of Abel. Better in volume, better in quality as well as better in vocabulary of expression. When one accepts the finished work of Christ on the cross of Calvary, their sins are blotted out by the blood of Jesus.

If you don't believe it, just read for yourself what Colossians 2:13-14 says about that.

Colossians; 2:13-14. ***And you, being dead in your sins and the uncircumcision of your***

> ***flesh, hath he quickened together with him, having forgiven you all trespasses.***
>
> ***14] Blotting out the handwriting of ordinances that was against us, which was contrary to us, and took it out of the way, nailing it to his cross.***

Those handwriting of ordinances that were against the sinner and that condemned the sinner, were first blotted out, taken out of the way, and then nailed to the cross of Christ's suffering.

4) The Applicability of Blood

Although the blood of Jesus was shed, notice that it doesn't work for just anybody. It works for only those over whom the blood of Jesus is applied. Remember in the land of Goshen, although the blood of the lamb was shed, it was only able to save the children of Israel over whose door post the blood was applied. In the Old Testament, the blood of bulls and goats were shed, but remember it was only when it was applied by the high priest upon the mercy seat that the sins of the people were atoned. The blood of Jesus can be the only substitute when an innocent blood is crying against you. But you must understand that although the blood is shed, it must be applied.

The Three Levels of Application of the Blood

You can know all there is to know about the blood of Jesus, but if you don't know how to apply the blood, you would not be able to experience total victory over sin and the devil. There are three levels of the application of the blood of Jesus.

1) *The blood must be applied God-ward*
2) *The blood must be applied Self-ward*
3) *The blood must be applied Satan-ward*

According to the ordinances of the Old Testament, once a year on the day of atonement, the High Priest will carry the blood bulls and goats and would make his way from the outer court, through the holy place and to the holy of hollies. Now notice that the holy of hollies doesn't have windows so there is no light in there.

- *The light in the outer court is sunlight because it is opened to the elements of the natural world.*
- *The light in the holy place, which does not have windows is candlelight.*
- *The light in the holy of hollies which also doesn't have windows is the Shekinah illumination.*

So immediately the High Priest steps into the darkness of the holy of hollies, then the shekinah descends into that place, and that is what provides illumination for the holy of hollies. In the event whereby the sins of the land supersede the nomenclature of the blood of bulls that was brought in that day for atonement, the high priest will die. That's why the coolest girdle was used to tie the waist of the high priest so that in case he dies in the holy of hollies he can be pulled out without any man having to enter the holy of hollies. In effect, the holy of hollies was a dangerous place and the only language that can be understood there was the language of blood, which no human being can understand or interpret.

5) Blood Has a Voice

Note that the voice of a guilty blood can be silenced but when innocent blood cries out, no voice nor any amount of prayer or fasting can ever silence it or shut it down until it is pacified.

Since Jesus was innocent of all the charges brought up against Him, His blood is an innocent blood as well as righteous, hence nothing in heaven or earth or under the sea could stop the cry of the innocent blood of Jesus. Nothing could stop the demands that the cry of His blood made to His heavenly father in the courts of heaven on our behalf and for the atonement of our sins. Therefore, whatsoever the innocent and righteous blood of Jesus demanded, God is ready and willing to grant it just like God granted to Abel when his innocent blood made demands for vengeance and justice against his brother Cain.

The blood of Jesus is the only substitute that can override the voice of an innocent blood crying against you. In the next chapter, I will delve into the subject of innocent blood and what it can accomplish when an innocent blood cries out to God. However, bear in mind that whenever an innocent blood cries out to God, God will respond with vengeance no matter how long it takes.

There are several examples in the bible including God's response to the innocent blood of Zachariah in the Old Testament. He was blamelessly killed between the porch and the altar of God while rendering priesthood duties unto God. Jesus clearly made this statement about that incident in Matthew 23:35.

> ***Upon you may come all the innocent blood shed on the earth, from the blood of innocent Abel to the blood of Zechariah, the son of Barachiah, whom Ye killed between the porch and the altar.***

It is worth noting that Jesus made this utterance to remind His stubborn and stiff-necked audience about the fact that no judgement will go unnoticed by God.

CHAPTER EIGHT

SOULS UNDER ALTAR

Revelation 6:9-11

9] And when he had opened the fifth seal, I saw under the altar the souls of them that were slain for the word of God, and for the testimony which they held:

10] And they cried with a loud voice, saying, How long, O Lord, holy and true, dost thou not judge and avenge our blood on them that dwell on the earth?

11] And white robes were given unto every one of them; and it was said unto them, that they should rest yet for a little season, until their fellowservants also and their brethren, that should be killed as † they were, should be fulfilled.

What did you expect the Christian life to be the day you raised your hands in the act of surround and invited Christ into your life? Did you think Christianity would be life on a bed of roses? Did you think it would be a cool day's walk in a park? Did you think this vile world would help you in any way to know God and live for Him? Did you think that the system of this world would still be friendly to you although it's programmed to be against God?

What was your expectation on how living for God would be?

A health and wealth gospel?

A name it and claim it promises?

A power of positive thinking outlook on life?

A feel-good religion that gives you warm fuzzy feelings?

A religion that consists of little more than everyone joining hands and singing "Kum-ba-yah My Lord kum -ba-yah"

A pre-tribulation rapture, sparing you from any form of persecution, or a golden-age era sparing you from suffering of any kind?

Revelation 6:9-11 sets before us a most sobering but realistic picture, as it provides answers to the questions above. If you want to know what you can expect in this Christian journey, I recommend you take some time and read through Revelation 6:9-11. If you think the opening of the first four seals in the book of revelation is disturbing, wait till you see what enfolds with the opening of the fifth seal and what it reveals! Also, if the riding forth of the four horsemen seem unsettling to you, wait till you see the unveiling of the fifth seal. When He opened the fifth seal, he said.

> ***I saw under the altar the souls of those who had been slain for the word of God and for the testimony which they held. (6:9).***

> ***Notice that as one makes his way through the book of Revelation, one will find that the imagery intensifies in that the images become more horrific, the scenes more terrifying and the issues more pressing.***

Brothers and sisters, ladies, and gentlemen, the fifth seal is opened and what we see are "souls under an altar". However, notice that these souls are not in possession of their bodies. We see only souls because their bodies were either buried in the ground somewhere, thrown into the sea, rotten and turned into worms upon the surface of the earth, eaten up by some wild beast or perished through whatever means by which they had died as Martyrs.

They are the souls of the Martyrs. These are those who have died through persecution while holding on to their most holy faith and refuse to recant or denounce Christ Jesus as their Savior. They are a representative fraction of the souls of those who have died a violent death and who are yet to die through similar horrific manner. These are the souls of those who had been stoned to death or beheaded over the centuries. Those who had been hanged, and sawn in two. These are the souls of those who had been burned as lamps to light up the arena in ancient Rome and other parts of the world. They are those who had been thrown to lions and other wild beast for their flesh to be eaten because they would not give up their faith in the Lord. They are those who have been counted as sheep for the slaughter according to Isaiah's prophesy. They represent the countless faithful who died because they held on to their testimony and sealed it with their own blood. They are all those who had died for the faith from the time of Christ's ascension till this very day.

For what reason had they been slain?

They had been slain simply because they held on to the word of God and to their most holy faith in the Lord and refused to recant, though it would eventually cost them their lives. If you want to know who some of these faithful are, one of them is the soul of Stephen, the first martyr in the New Testament. His soul is there under the altar. The souls of the early apostles of Jesus Christ are also there under the altar. For instance, Church History has it that each of the twelve disciples of Jesus, except for Judas Iscariot who took his own life after betraying Jesus and John the revelator who died a Martyr in the Island of Patmos.

Church history has it that.

> *Peter - was crucified upside down with his legs and feet up and head pointing downwards.*
>
> *James - was beheaded at Jerusalem.*
>
> *Andrew - was crucified on an X-shaped cross.*
>
> *Nathanael - was beheaded.*
>
> *Matthew - was killed by a sword driven through his body.*

Thomas - was run through with a spear.

The other James (not James the brother of John) - was thrown from a tower, stoned, and then sawn in pieces.

Judas - (not Judas Iscariot), was shot to death with arrows.

Paul - was most likely beheaded.

The soul of Polycarp, one of the early church fathers who died a Martyr at the age of 86, is also there under the altar. When he was threatened with wild beasts, he said, "*Bring them on!*" When he was threatened with fire, he said, "Burn me if you will, you threaten me with fire, the pains of which last for an hour, but the pains of eternal fire await you!" He was burned at the stake and did not recant his faith in the Lord Jesus Christ. I can tell you his soul is also there under the altar.

History has it that there was a 15-year-old slave girl named Blandina. She was tortured with every torture known to men and yet would not recant her faith in Christ. She was burned upon a hot iron chair and would not recant. She was suspended from a stake as food for the wild beasts and the beasts would not touch her body. She was finally placed in a net and thrown to a wild bull, which tore apart and devoured her little body. History has it that because her persistence annoyed the pagans who persecuted her, although she was dead yet in their anger, they drove a dagger through her lifeless body. The blood-thirsty mob in the amphitheater had never seen such courage. People were astonished at the slave girl's victorious cry even during her pain and suffering. She said, "I am a Christian and there is nothing vile done by us". Even though the crowd detested these Christians, they had to admit that never had a woman endured so much pain and terrible tortures as Blandina did. History has it that the pagans swore on that day that never had they seen a woman suffer with such courage as Blandina. The soul of Blandina is also there under the altar crying for the vengeance of our God.

John Huss was burn at the stake and so was English bible translator William Tyndale. Their soul together with countless others are still crying under the altar for the vengeance of our God. Notice that the souls of the number of those perishing for the faith is being added daily even until today throughout many parts of the world. The last century has been a century of persecution in which more Christians died for their faith than in all the previous centuries combined.

- *In 1915, Turkish authorities killed over 600,000 Armenians, most of them Christians. The souls of those martyrs are there under the altar too.*
- *In communist Russia; Lenin said, "there can be nothing more abominable than religion," and he ordered the persecution of countless Russian Orthodox churches and their members.*
- *Joseph Stalin extended that persecution to all believers and as a result, thousands of Christians were killed for the faith. The souls of those innocent martyrs are there under the altar.*
- *In 1956 the Auca Indians of Ecuador killed Missionaries Jim Elliot, Pete Fleming, Ed McCulley, Roger Younderian, and Nate Saint who had gone there to share the gospel of*

Jesus Christ with them. The souls of those martyrs are there too under the altar.

- *Ten thousand Cambodian Christians were slain in 1975. The souls of those martyrs are there under the altar crying for vengeance as well.*
- *What about the Christians slain in communist China, and Islamic stronghold of Indonesia, Iran and many more countries. The souls of those martyrs are there too.*

Take note of where John sees the souls of the martyrs? He sees them under the altar. Why under an altar? Because during the days of the temple worship there were in Jerusalem two altars.

1) the altar of burnt sacrifice and
2) the altar of incense.

It is worth noting that the altar that John the Revelator saw does not represent the altar of incense that stood in the Holy Place just before the curtains of the Holy of Holies. It cannot be because no blood is shed at the altar of incense. The altar John saw represent the altar of burnt sacrifice that stood in the outer court and upon which the animals were sacrificed, their blood being poured out at the bottom of the altar. Notice that this is the altar by which they enter the presence of God because remember it's located in the outer court, and the outer court is the point of entry into the temple.

That's why the Apostle Paul said in Philippians 3:10-11.

> ***10] That I may know him, and the power of his resurrection, and the fellowship of his sufferings, being made conformable unto his death.***

11] If by any means I might attain unto the resurrection of the dead.

The kind of fellowship that the Apostle Paul is referring to is not the type to share a drink, dine together, or make merry. It is a fellowship of suffering that confers upon born-again believers their identification with Christ. Notice therefore that in the place where you would see the blood of the sacrifice on the Old Testament altar, you now see the souls of the martyrs according to Revelation 6.

The altar of sacrifice, the altar of the cross, the altar of suffering, the altar of pain, the altar of persecution and the altar of self-denial is that through which every one of us at some point in our Christian walk with God would have to enter through if indeed we truly mean to make it into God's presence someday.

This is because their blood has been poured out, as they had sealed their faith in death. That is the scene set before us in the opening of the fifth seal. This represents the souls of all the martyrs who had died for the faith, from the time of Christ's ascension till the time of His glorious return in the clouds to rapture the New Testament church which is still an event in the future.

The Cry of the Martyrs

These martyrs cried out in verse 10:

And they cried with a loud voice, saying, 'How long, O Lord, holy and true, until

> ***You judge and avenge our blood on those who dwell on the earth?***

This is a cry of innocent blood for vengeance since it is the cry of those who had already been slain. It is the cry of souls in heaven and not of Christians on earth. Therefore, the soul of Stephen the first martyr in the New Testament in heaven today cries out ***"How long, O Lord, holy and true, until You judge and avenge our blood on those who dwell on the earth?"***

But notice that was not Stephen's cry in martyrdom. When they were stoning Stephen to death in the flesh, at the time his cry was, ***"Lord, do not charge them with this sin.*** This is because in his death, he was conformed to his Savior Jesus Christ who also cried in the same manner on the cross: "***Father, forgive them, for they know not what they do!"***

Remember what Philippians 3:10 said.

> **10]** ***That I may know him, and the power of his resurrection, and the fellowship of his sufferings, being made "conformable unto his death.***

At times we are tempted to curse our enemies and those that persecute us, but the lesson God is teaching us in this text is that, in persecution and in suffering you cannot curse or cry any other cry besides the cry of our chief martyr who cried on the cross and said - Father forgive them, for they know not what they do.

In suffering, in persecution, and yes, even in death, the cry of the martyr must conform to the cry of the Lord of all martyrs who is Our Lord Jesus Christ. That's why the bible speaks about being conformable unto his death.

So, in death Stephen's cry had to conform to the cry of our Lord and savior Jesus Christ. However, now as a martyr under the altar he cries; ***How long, O Lord, holy and true, until You judge and avenge our blood on those who dwell on the earth?***

Notice the change in his cry after death. Why the change in his cry. It is because under the altar, the souls of these martyrs stand in glory and their cry is based not on the redeeming grace of Jesus Christ but rather on the character of God as righteous judge of all. So, notice that under the altar they call God "Lord", and God is rightly so because He has absolute power and authority. They also call Him *"holy and true"*, because in His holiness and truth, He must judge the sinner and the wicked. This He will certainly do because He has said in His word, ***vengeance is Mine sayest the Lord; For I will repay.***

Also notice that God is not quite about their cry. See the Lord's response in Revelation 6:11

> ***Then a white robe was given to each of them; and it was said to them that they should rest a little while longer, until both the number of their fellow servants and their brethren, who would be killed as they were, was completed.***

The souls of these martyrs are comforted by the Lord's response and given a white robe and commanded to rest. The white robe represents the righteousness of Christ. They have been liberated by Christ, consecrated by Christ, crowned by the Lamb in the righteousness of the Lamb and they rest enjoying eternal Sabbatical rest. Therefore, although justice is delayed but justice is not and will never be denied. This is because final judgment has not yet been poured out upon their enemies, which are also the enemies of the cross and of Christ. Though they stand clothed in the righteousness of Christ Jesus. Though these martyrs already enjoy Sabbatical rest, they anxiously await the final judgment when the quick and the dead shall all be judged.

When then shall judgement come

John tells us in Revelation 6 that they should rest a little while longer, until both the number of their fellow servants and their brethren, who would be killed as they were, was completed. Don't you find this phrase disturbing. Don't you find it unsettling. You should if you are not! What this is saying to us is that there are many more yet to be killed even in our day as these martyrs were killed in the past. And so here we are called fellow servants and brothers of these souls under the altar because some of us who are alive today are also going to face our own persecution, suffering, torture, and agony of soul, or even death for the sake of the gospel and for our faith in the Lord.

A Theologian once said; "The days on God's calendar are marked off, one by one, in the

blood of the martyrs. What this means is that, on God's calendar, He measures the time until the judgment by the blood of the martyrs!"

Meaning, your blood or mine could very well run alongside theirs. I hope you get the point being carried across by this saying. God has ordained that the judgment due these souls under the altar, will not come until the number of the martyrs be complete, and that may include any of us at any point in time.

The bible says, in ***Hebrews 12:3-4.***

> 3] ***For consider him that endured such contradiction of sinners against himself, lest ye be wearied and faint in your minds.***
>
> ***4] Ye have not yet resisted unto blood, striving against sin. (AMP. Version)***

Hebrews 11:38

> ***Women received their dead raised to life again: †: and others were tortured, not accepting deliverance; that they might obtain a better resurrection:***
>
> ***And others had trial of cruel mockings and scourgings, yea, moreover of bonds and imprisonment:***

> ***They were stoned, they were sawn asunder, were tempted, were slain with the sword: †: they wandered about in sheepskins and goatskins; †; being destitute, afflicted, tormented.***
>
> ***(Of whom the world was not worthy:) they wandered in deserts, and in mountains, and in dens and caves of the earth.***

Hebrews 12:1

> ***Seeing we also are compassed about † with so great a cloud of witnesses, let us lay aside every weight, and the sin which doth so easily beset us, and let us run with patience the race that is set before us.***

Notice that the presence of the witnesses mentioned in Hebrews 12:1 is very important because these are men and women who lived in the flesh like we are doing now and were faced with same, similar, or even tougher circumstances of life and yet did not give up on their faith but rather stood their grounds even unto death. Beginning with Stephen as the first martyr of the New Testament era. When Stephen died as the first martyr, it was a lonely cry. But then, the cry of the apostles soon joined his cry. And the souls of the early Christians soon joined the cry of the apostles. And the cry of the Reformers soon joined the cry of the early Christians. And the cries of those who have died in the last century has joined the cry of the Reformers and the list goes on and on together, building a great army of martyrs.

We have become a generation that's full of excuses because we cannot serve God in purity and holiness in our day. Some day when you stand before the Lord with excuses for reasons why you may have given up on your faith in the Lord, the cloud of witnesses mentioned in the word of God will step into the witnesses stand and testify against you based on the fact that they also endured similar or worse persecutions for their faith but still stood our grounds and were found faithful to the end.

Think about it!, the souls of all the martyrs who have died for the word of God and for the testimony of their faith from the time of the Ascension of Christ till this very day, and to this very moment are crying out under the altar in heaven: ***How long, O Lord, holy and true, until You judge and avenge our blood on those who dwell on the earth?***

Therefore, do you think the cries of these martyrs are going to be ignored or fall on deaf ears. Do you think these cries are going to pass by unnoticed by the righteous judge of all. These are the cry of souls for whom Christ died. These are the cry of souls for whom the Lamb of God gave His life. These are the cry of those who have been purchased by the blood of the Lamb. These are the cry of those who have been loved by the Lamb with an everlasting love! Do you think the cry of the innocent blood of these martyrs would not be heard and avenged by the righteous judge. For a moment just consider the following scenarios.

- *They stoned Stephen and thought that Jesus Christ, the Cornerstone, would remain silent.*
- *They threw the Christians to the lions and thought that the Lion of the Tribe of Judah would remain silent.*
- *They burned Christians at the stake and thought that He whose eyes are like flames of fire would remain silent.*
- *They thrust Christians through with the sword and thought that He who will strike the nations with the sword out of His mouth would remain silent.*

O How foolish is the wicked in thinking that God will be silent forever. If all these souls under the altar went through all these suffering for their faith, this then is what one can expect as a faithful believer in Jesus Christ. You can expect persecution. You can expect suffering. You can expect torture. You can expect even death. It is a most sobering and realistic picture of a life that's fully yielded to Christ without any reservation. This is a perfect example of the faithful of whom the bible described in Revelation 12:11 as people who overcame Satan and evil, and who did not love their lives unto death.

> ***And they overcame him by the blood of the Lamb, and by the word of their testimony; and they loved not their lives unto the death.***
> **Revelation 12:11 KJV**:

What we need as believers to stand firm and strong in these last days is true faith in Jesus Christ, because true faith clings to Christ in persecution. True faith clings to Christ in suffering. True faith clings to Christ in death. The Apostle Paul says in Romans 8:36a-39, ***we are accounted as sheep***

for the slaughter. Nay, in all these things we are more than conquerors through him that loved us.

> ***For I am persuaded, that neither death, nor life, nor angels, nor principalities, nor powers, nor things present, nor things to come,***
>
> ***Nor height, nor depth, nor any other creature, shall be able to separate us from the love of God, which is in Christ Jesus our Lord.***

Do you have a made-up mind today. Note that whatsoever is having a pull on your life isn't worth the eternal price of your soul. Make up your mind to stand and do stand by the grace of God until Christ' return.

CHAPTER NINE

WHEN INNOCENT BLOOD CRIES

As a well-known fact, the bible is made up of both the Old and the New Testaments. However, notice that there is no fulfillment in the New Testament without the Old Testament. Likewise, there is no blessing in the New Testament without the Old Testament. As an example, one can see a connection between the death of Christ and the blessings of Father Abraham when the bible declared that ***Curse be everyone that hung on the tree, that the blessings of Abraham might come upon the Gentiles.*** What this teaches us is that the blessings that we are experiencing in the New Testament, are Old Testament in nature. They are ancestral in nature through Abraham who lived over 6000 years ago.

If what happened in the past has no bearing on the present, then why did Jesus have to come and die for sins inherited from Adam which occurred in the past.

There are many Christians that strange things happens to from time to time. This includes sudden death, repetitive circumstances in their lives, curses related to bloodline, and more. One may wonder how come things of such nature do at times happen to born-again, water baptized, Holy Ghost filled believers. This subject is not one of the common or regular subjects that one may hear being taught or preached from the pulpit on Sundays, however I want to use these out-of-place circumstances to expound on what happens when innocent blood cries. While the voice of guilty blood can be overpowered, on the other hand, when innocent blood cries, there is a lot more to it. At times and under certain circumstances, blood is shed as guilty blood. For example, when people get killed while doing some evil deed, they die in their sins and the blood shed is associated with guilt. Should that happen, the shedding of their blood is different from when innocent blood is shed.

Sometimes, the issues that are repetitive and never seem to go away in the lives of individuals or that runs through families may be due to innocent blood that's crying out against an individual through evil deeds perpetuated in their bloodline. The situations that never seem to go away are sometimes due to some evil deed that was carried out in the bloodline of a family and hence causing innocent blood that is shed to cry out for justice and appeasement. According to II Samuel 21, at one point in time there was famine in Israel year after year, and David began to suspect that something must be wrong because of the repetitive nature of the famine. Hence, he decided to enquire of the Lord concerning what might possibly be the cause for the repetitive famine in the land. The Lord answered David and indicated that it was because King Saul had slew many Gibeonites with whom the children of Israel during their journey out of Egypt, had come into a peace covenant with dating as far back to the time of Joshua *(the backdrop story is in Joshua 9- the interlude to the conquest of Canaan).*

In Joshua 9:14, Joshua and the Elders of the tribes of Israel made a league (covenant) or a peace treaty as one may call it today with the Gibeonites before they came to the knowledge that these Gibeonites were deceptive and that they had deceived Israel about their origin. However, because the covenant was sealed in the name of the Lord of Host, it could not be reversed. Therefore, since they couldn't reverse the covenant, Joshua made a pronouncement upon the Gibeonites, and he said that they shall be hewers of wood and drawers of water for the congregation of Israel and for the altar of the Lord. While this may seem like a curse in the physical sense, on the other hand, it made them the Gibeonites spiritually attached to the house of Israel hence their safety and wellbeing became a responsibility of Israel.

As a result, in the battle of Ajalon, although the battle was not Israel's battle. It was directly aimed at the Gibeonites for joining themselves to Israel, but because of the peace covenant that had been made between Israel and the Gibeonites, God had to fight for the Gibeonites through the hand of the armies of Israel. That's how powerful covenants are. They are binding once entered, and especially so when it's done in the name of the Lord.

Many are those who are of the opinion that once you get saved, that's the end of all that was done in your lineage through blood guilt, but this story teaches us that contrary to this opinion held by many, the evils committed through one's bloodline can affect the lives of people generations to come even if they were not direct partakers of those evil deeds.

The blood of our direct ancestors still runs through our veins hence we cannot biologically nor spiritually dissociate ourselves from them. The reason why this is a mystery is because it has to do with blood.

From this story, we can also learn that this notion is not true because consider that fact that God stood by unconcern while Ahimelech and the 85 priest who were Israelites were slain, but God spoke out vehemently when the Gibeonites who are strangers were killed. What makes the difference in these two scenarios is the covenant that was entered into between Israel and the Gibeonites. Covenants by their nature and spiritual significance, are such a powerful that once entered, it cannot be brushed off under the pretense that they never existed.

The Spirit of a fugitive

Bible says when Christ died, sinners were redeemed from the curse of the law and sin, but exactly what type of curse were sinners redeemed from, since the bible makes it clear that there are different type of curses.

- *We have the curse of sin – which was inherited through Adam.*
- *The curse as a result non-observance of the law - that curse was for Israel.*
- *The curse of the vagabond – that was for Cain. God told Cain that; "a fugitive and a vagabond shall Ye be" and that's a curse.*

Genesis 4:12a ***"When thou tillest the ground, it shall not henceforth yield unto thee her strength"*** *- that's also a curse to humankind after the fall in the garden of Eden.*

God said to Cain, what is it that thou has done. The blood of thy brother is crying from the ground to me. Notice that Cain's curse was due to blood guilt. That's the cry of an innocent blood. It never shuts up nor ceases to cry out until it's dealt with. It is worth noting that the first sin ever committed was the sin of treason. That was to make man disobey God by eating of the fruit that the Lord had commanded Adam not to eat in the garden of Eden (Genesis 3:8). Sin would always want to push you from where God places you if you entertain it and allow it to take a hold in your life. It was sin that pushed Adam away not God, and it was sin that drive Cain to the land of Nod, not God.

The second sin of humankind, however, was to make man touch blood, and that was through the murder committed by Cain. As a result, he was cursed by the earth;

A fugitive shall thou be upon the surface of the earth.

Notice that the spirit of a fugitive is an unrest spirit. That's why Cain became restless after that curse was pronounced upon his life. Restlessness is one of the leading causes of violence in our society today. When people are restless, they tend to think that their plight is due to their location, so they restlessly move from one place to another, thinking that the new place would make them feel better than the former, only to find out that the problem is not with the place but rather it is with the condition of their heart toward God. Restless people usually eliminate God from their thoughts and hence that gives room for other spirits to take control of their thoughts and eventually of their lives. Restlessness is the spirit of a fugitive and that was exactly the nature of Cain's curse '*a fugitive shall thou be upon the surface of the earth*.

While the first sin ever committed had to do with disobedience, notice however that the second had to do with the shedding of innocent blood.

Notice that Cain's punishment was not to become an ordinary fugitive. It's fugitive by reason of a curse and on purpose. It's possible to find such people even in church. They move from one church to another, from one city, town, or village to another, from one job, line of profession, or business to another and they are always restless and on the move because a fugitive spirit has been cast upon their lives and hence begin to live under the shadows of a restless spirit. King Saul was in his right mind until he disobeyed the command of God to kill all the Amalekites in battle. As a result, a restless spirit took control over his life. When King Saul disobeyed God and he was removed by God from the throne of Israel, the bible says an unclean spirit came to indwell Saul. If you notice that spirit turned Saul into a very restless man from that time forward. His restlessness caused him to want to kill David without a cause. It also caused him to kill several Gibeonites without a justified cause and to commit many atrocities before his death. When King Saul killed the Gibeonites, innocent blood was shed, and that blood, because it's innocent, cried out unto God for vengeance. God heard their cry, and at the beginning of the reign of David, God responded with a famine upon the land of Israel.

Restlessness is one of the leading causes of violence in our society today. When people are restless, they usually attribute it to causes related to their environment. However, restlessness has more to do with the condition of a man's heart than it has to do with their location.

It hasn't been written in the bible that those who put their trust in the Lord shall cast our young; so why is it that for many Christian couples, although they may be committed Christians yet keep having miscarriage every time they try to have children.? Could it be that there could be some blood guilt in the bloodline of such a family which has become the source of the problem? One may have blood guilt on their hands and yet they may born-again believers and may wonder how that is possible. The common signs of blood guilt in families includes but not limited to repetitive barrenness, miscarriages, sudden death, and some genetic illnesses and mental disorders, just to name a few. It could be the cause of poverty in other families. It could yet be the cause of some notable diseases or peculiar and predominant health conditions that runs through generations in some families.

As an example, when one commits abortion, abortion is just the medical term, but the actual act is referred to as murder in the bible because it has to do with the shedding of innocent blood hence it becomes blood guilt in the person's family or bloodline. By so doing, one establishes an altar of sacrifice that will always demand blood through generations to come in that family. That's why although people may have left childbearing, yet the innocent blood that they may have shed through abortions are demanding blood from their daughters, grand-daughters, and great grand-daughters, and hence the reason for repetitive miscarriages in such families.

Do not underestimate what the presence of blood guilt in families could lead to and how long it can run through generations of a family.

The comparison between guilty blood and innocent blood is a very interesting subject to explore. I will therefore like to expound on the mystery surrounding both guilty and innocent blood and why although guilty blood has a voice which can be stopped, but on the other hand the cry of an innocent blood cannot be stopped, nor ignored not even by prayer or any other means until it's appeased through the right manner. This has to do with spiritual equity and justice.

I will begin with the story of David and Ahimelech the priest. When David was on the run away from King Saul, he went to consult Ahimelech the priest for help. While David was with Ahimelech, a man by name Doeg (pronounced Do-e.g.) who was loyal to King Saul, saw David leaving the presence of Ahimelech and he went and told King Saul about the meeting between David and Ahimelech. King Saul in his anger, commanded that Ahimelech and all the 85 priest who serve under him should be killed because they had received David and entertained his presence with them. Out of reverence, the soldiers who were with the king did not want to touch these priests because of their reverence for God and the fact that these priests were those who serve day and night before the God in the temple. But this stranger by name Doeg who had no reverence for God, went on a slaughter and killed all the 85 priests at the command of King Saul. The only one among the 85 priest who managed to escape the slaughter is a priest name Abiatha (I Samuel 22;20).

The question then is, why would God stand by unconcern while his priest who wear the linen ephod were being slain by a stranger and God did not act in their defense, as if God was not concern about their wellbeing or safety.

Why would the God of Israel stand by unconcerned while 85 priest who serve before the altar of God were slain and yet He moved in haste to defend the Gibeonites whose forefathers were slain by King Saul.

Yet when the Gibeonites who are by the way, strangers to the commonwealth of Israel and who by deception made a peace covenant with Israel dating as far back as the time of Joshua were killed, God acted in displeasure by sending drought and famine year after year upon the land of Israel. It seem strange why God seem unconcern about the killing of His priest and yet will act in defense of strangers who were killed. It's because although the 85 priest were innocently killed, (1 Samuel 3) but it's also worth noting that there was already a death sentence over their head because of the sins of Eli and of the sons of Eli.

The 85 priest who were killed were descendants of Ichabod the son of one of the two sons of Eli who took bribes and lay with women in the gates of the temple and both of whom died in battle on the same day because of God's judgement upon the house of Eli. Because of God's judgement for their actions, God had Sworn unto the house of Eli in I Samuel 3:14 that "***The iniquity of Eli's house shall not be purged with sacrifice nor offering forever***".

This was a serious indictment upon both the house of Eli and the descendants of Eli. As a result, the 85 priests who were direct descendants of Eli were killed and God stood by and did not act so His word could be fulfill exactly as was spoken against the house of Eli. Secondly, according to I Samuel 2:31 there was another curse pronounced against the house of Eli. ***"There shall not be an old man in thy house.... for they shall die in the prime of their age"***.

When David died, Solomon said to Abiatha, (the only one who managed escaped the slaughter of the 85 priest) ***"bring thy linen ephod and give it to Zadok and go to thy house and hide thy self. If you come out from your house, your blood will be upon your head"***.

King Solomon took this course of action because Abiatha was part of the descendants of Eli who should have died in the slaughter of the 85 priests but managed to escape the sword of Doeg.

CHAPTER TEN

BLOOD GUILT

Guilty Blood

While blood can be referred to as being an innocent blood, others can be referred to as guilty blood. A blood guilt is the condemnation that comes upon a man, woman, a couple, a clan, a tribe, or even a nation because of the shedding of innocent blood. This is so because an innocent blood will keep crying for divine justice and until it's appeased in a proper manner, no amount of prayer, fasting, binding, and loosing will be able to shut down its voice down. Back to II Sam 21, the bible says when innocent blood is shed, that blood will continue to cry until that blood is appeased.

I was told of a story about a brilliant young Ghanaian medical student who used his college hostel room to perform abortions for female students on campus who wanted to terminate pregnancies. He did this to earn his living on campus. It was said that one day he had a dream that the world had come to an end, and he was on his way to heaven. As he stepped one foot into the gates of heaven, the other foot will not come up. He struggled to pull the other foot up until he turn to see what was hindering and preventing his other foot from stepping up. To his surprise, when he looked down, he saw that his foot was tied to a rope held by human hands and on the lower part of the rope was several babes representing the souls of babies killed through all the pregnancies that he had helped to terminate through abortion whiles he was a medical student on campus. In the dream he said every one of those babies were railing accusations against him and questioning him about why he did not give them the chance to live. Some said, "they were destined to be someone great, but he took away their lives from them". Others said, "they were supposed to be someone great in life, but he did not give them a chance to live nor taste of life on earth because he aborted them before their entry into the world".

If there is any sin that is gradually pulling America as a nation back from its position of prominence on the world stage, it is the sin of blood guilt. America is gradually losing her grip on the world stage as a world power and world leader. The leading cause of this drift from global prominence and power is because of America's involvement with abortion of babies. Any nation under the sun whose laws support the shedding of innocent blood, brings upon herself a curse.

Blood guilt is the condemnation that comes upon a man, woman, a couple, a family, clan, tribe, or even a nation because of the shedding of innocent blood. The seriousness of blood guilt is that it's consequences could last through several generations until the

appropriate spiritual measures are taken to stop it.

According to Leviticus 18:25-28

And thou shalt not let any of thy seed pass through the fire to Molech, neither shalt thou profane the name of thy God: I am the LORD.

The above scripture is in reference to offering their children in blood sacrifices unto the gods of the land of Canaan. Today, America is doing the same but in a different form, by offering babies as blood sacrifice through the abortion of babies. The consequences of blood sacrifices is that the land becomes defiled because God visits the iniquities thereof upon the land. But that's not the end of the consequences.

[25] And the land is defiled: therefore, I do visit the iniquity thereof upon it, and the land itself vomiteth out her inhabitants.

The verse 25 above says, furthermore the land itself vomits or spues out her inhabitants and this I would say, is a serious indictment against America as a nation. (Verse 28)

[26] Ye shall therefore keep my statutes and my judgments, and shall not commit any of these abominations; neither any of your own nation, nor any stranger that sojourneth among you:

> [27] ***(For all these abominations have the men of the land done, which were before you, and the land is defiled;)***
>
> [28] ***That the land spue not you out also, when ye defile it, as it spued out the nations that were before you.***

The Story of Cain and Abel in fourth chapter of Genesis is a good example of the detrimental impacts of blood guilt upon an individual or upon a land.

Genesis 4:1-16

> ***4 And Adam knew Eve his wife; and she conceived, and bare Cain, and said, I have gotten a man from the LORD.***
>
> [2] ***And she again bare his brother Abel. And Abel was a keeper of sheep, but Cain was a tiller of the ground.***
>
> [3] ***And in process of time it came to pass, that Cain brought of the fruit of the ground an offering unto the LORD.***
>
> [4] ***And Abel, he also brought of the firstlings of his flock and of the fat thereof. And the LORD had respect unto Abel and to his offering:***

[5] But unto Cain and to his offering he had not respect. And Cain was very wroth, and his countenance fell.

[6] And the LORD said unto Cain, Why art thou wroth? and why is thy countenance fallen?

[7] If thou doest well, shalt thou not be accepted? and if thou doest not well, sin lieth at the door. And unto thee shall be his desire, and thou shalt rule over him.

[8] And Cain talked with Abel his brother: and it came to pass, when they were in the field, that Cain rose up against Abel his brother, and slew him.

[9] And the LORD said unto Cain, Where is Abel thy brother? And he said, I know not: Am I my brother's keeper?

[10] And he said, What hast thou done? the voice of thy brother's blood crieth unto me from the ground.

[11] And now art thou cursed from the earth, which hath opened her mouth to receive thy brother's blood from thy hand;

[12] When thou tillest the ground, it shall not henceforth yield unto thee her strength; a

fugitive and a vagabond shalt thou be in the earth.

[13] ***And Cain said unto the LORD, My punishment is greater than I can bear.***

[14] ***Behold, thou hast driven me out this day from the face of the earth; and from thy face shall I be hid; and I shall be a fugitive and a vagabond in the earth; and it shall come to pass, that every one that findeth me shall slay me.***

[15] ***And the LORD said unto him, Therefore whosoever slayeth Cain, vengeance shall be taken on him sevenfold. And the LORD set a mark upon Cain, lest any finding him should kill him.***

[16] ***And Cain went out from the presence of the LORD, and dwelt in the land of Nod, on the east of Eden.***

It is very interesting to note from the verse 11 that when Cain shed innocent blood by killing is brother, it was not God who cursed Cain. It was the earth that cursed Cain.

God said to Cain; ***And now art thou cursed "from the earth", which has opened her mouth to receive thy brother's blood from thy hand.***

Notice that the curse came from the earth and not from God. Therefore, five lessons that can be learnt from the above statement made by God.

- *The earth is a living creature not a dead creature.*
- *The earth has a mouth.*
- *The earth is referred to as 'her.'*
- *The earth can bring forth meaning what the earth has in common with the female is a womb.*
- *The earth can hear because it heard what was spoken.*

The earth, which is living cursed Cain because the earth doesn't like to drink blood and for that matter and innocent blood. Hence, every time innocent blood is shed upon the earth, the earth is forced to drink the blood of the innocent and as a result, the earth releases curses upon both the individuals and the bloodlines of the individuals who shed innocent blood as well as upon the land. These are a few attributes of the earth that the believer needs to pay attention to.

- The earth is a living creature
- The earth has mouth
- The earth is a 'she' and hence it brings forth and like a woman, it has a womb.
- The earth as ears because it heard God's command from the beginning of creation to 'bring forth' and it did exactly that.

Notice that is why the bible addresses the earth and woman in the same way. It is because the earth and the woman God created, both has a lot in common.

As an example.

- *The earth can be barren, and the woman can also be barren*
- *The earth brings forth and the woman also brings forth.*
- *The earth is referred to as "her" and the woman is also 'her.'*
- *The earth is mother, and the woman is also a mother.*
- *The earth has a womb, and the woman also has a womb.*
- *Seeds are sown into the earth and seed are also sown into a woman in terms of reproduction.*

Iniquity is the type of sin that needs to be taken very seriously because unlike transgressions, iniquity imparts a bloodline and affects several generations to come. There is a difference between sin, transgression, and iniquity as noted in previous chapters of this book. When one shed innocent blood, it's beyond sin and transgression. It elevates to iniquity. In the Old Testament, when a man kills another man, blood is not only required from the killer but also from the brother of the killer even if the brother is innocent.

When you have a problem that is repetitive in nature, sometimes it's due to blood guilt. In 11 Samuel 3:21, why is it that the famine mentioned was repetitive and continued for a period of three years. Perhaps, it wouldn't have stopped without David's enquiry and God's intervention. It's obvious that if King David did not take steps to enquire of the Lord, the famine would have gone on even far more than three years. Signs of blood guilt in families can include but not limited to lack of stability, repetitive sins, reoccurrence of peculiar situation, trends of sudden death in families and more. When innocent blood is crying for appeasement, no voice can over-ride it's cry in prayer or in fasting.

In II Samuel 3 what was the solution in the case of the famine mentioned?. The Gibeonites, who were slaves are now seem making demands upon the King of Israel. David was therefore obligated to do for them whatever they requested of him for the famine to cease. They said they wanted the direct blood of the one who shed the blood of our ancestors. So, they requested for seven direct descendants of King Saul to be hanged. Hence King David had to issue instructions for seven sons of Saul to be hanged because they wanted the blood of Saul, but because Saul was dead, they substituted it for the blood of the sons of Saul. This includes the two sons of Rizpah who use to be a concubine of King Saul. When they were looking for seven men of the direct lineage of King Saul, they added Rizpah's two sons to make up the number although Rizpah was only a concubine to King Saul.

Micah didn't give birth, but Saul's daughter married a man, and they took the five sons she had with this man as part of the seven and hanged them. Two sons of Rizpah, Saul's concubine were also killed to make up the number because they had the blood of Saul in them. It's worth noting that although Micah did not give birth but had a sister who had five children and their blood was taken because the blood of Saul was in them. The only reason why they couldn't touch Mephibosheth although he was a direct descendent of King Saul, was because of the covenant that existed between David and Jonathan the father of Mephibosheth. That goes to show how powerful covenants are.

May the blood of Jesus speak for us no matter what innocent blood is crying against us because of the iniquities of our fathers. Remember I mentioned earlier that when innocent blood cries, it doesn't stop until it's appeased. Noticed that immediately after the blood of the sons of Saul were shed, God entreated King David and Israel and the famine ceased.

I don't have a great heritage because when you come from a royal family in Africa, it's the place of shedding of innocent blood more than anywhere else on the continent. When innocent blood is crying, it can only be silence with the blood of Jesus, but you first must identify yourself with the iniquities of the fathers and seek God's forgiveness on their behalf. That is putting yourself in their place and standing in the gap for their sins to be pardoned. Beside blood, another mystery is the pouring of libation, which is a subject that I will expound in future writings.

It is interesting to note that God in His infinite wisdom, made sure that Satan played a critical role in having Christ crucified.

1. By working through Judas to betray Christ.
2. By working through the men who paid Judas to delivered Jesus.
3. By working behind the scenes through those who cheered-on Barabbas so he will be freed instead of Jesus the sinless lamb of God.
4. And ultimately by working through the Roman authorities who drove the nails into Jesus' hands, feet, and side.

Notice that when Satan helped killed Jesus, Satan shed an innocent blood because Jesus was innocent of all the charges, they railed against him. Hence because the blood of Jesus was an innocent blood as well as righteous, the moment the first drops of His blood touched the earth, the cry of His blood went up to God in heaven. Like the innocent blood of Abel, it started to cry unto God and when it cried God heard because it's an innocent blood and whatever that blood demanded for appeasement that was what God will do.

But unlike the blood of Abel which demanded vengeance against his brother Cain, instead of the blood of Jesus demanding vengeance as a reward for the shedding of His innocent blood the blood of Jesus rather demanded for the release of all the captives. The ones who are guilty of Sin from the time of Adam throughout the ages until present time. Therefore, the innocent blood of Jesus demanded both the pardon and the release of all who had sin against God and were deserving of death since the wages for their sins was death. That included the sins of even those that pierced him and nailed him to the cross of Calvary when he said, *"father forgive them; for they know not what they do"*.

CHAPTER ELEVEN

BLOOD OF SPRINKLING

Hebrews 12:22-24

> ***22 But ye have come unto Mount Zion and unto the city of the living God, the heavenly Jerusalem, and to an innumerable company of angels,***
>
> ***23 to the general assembly and church of the firstborn, who are written in Heaven, and to God the Judge of all, and to the spirits of just men made perfect,***
>
> ***24 and to Jesus the Mediator of the new covenant, and to the blood of sprinkling, that speaketh better things than that of Abel.***

The verse 24 makes it very clear that the blood of Jesus speaketh *'Better'* things than that of Abel.

1. **Better in Quality**

The use of the word "better" denotes a comparison between the blood of Jesus and that of Abel. When a thing is described as better, it obviously implies it being compared to one that is good but of a lesser value or quality. Hence the English language has good, better, and best.

> ***"Better" does not negate the fact that the blood of Abel is also speaking, but rather the fact that what the blood of Jesus is speaking is a higher quality than that of Abel.***

Better as used does not negate the fact that the blood of Abel is also speaking, but rather the fact that what the blood of Abel is saying has lesser ability, lesser potency, and lesser power as compared to what the blood of Jesus is speaking. Therefore, although the blood of Abel is speaking, it is not speaking things that are good enough compared to that of Jesus.

2. **Better in volume**

This means the blood of Jesus speak better in the sense that it is higher in volume. The volume at which the blood of Abel is speaking is overpowered and absorbed by the volume of the blood of Jesus, so that the when the volume of one voice overpowers, overshadows, and ultimately consumes the volume of the other, it is as if the one overshadowed or consumed ceases to exist or becomes of any relevance.

For example, when a child or a babe is crying, because their voice is low in volume, the voice of an adult speaking through a microphone connected to a powered amplified system or instrument can totally swallow up the volume of the voice of the babe to such an extent that one would not be able to hear the sound of the voice coming from the baby because of the volume of the adult voice is over-powering, and overwhelms the volume of the voice of the baby. For instance, in the days of old and according to the culture of the Canaanites and other heathen nations which practice idol worship, when they are offering babies as sacrifice unto their gods by casting the babies into fire, to appease their conscious or for whatever reason, they do not want to hear the voice of the babies screaming in the fire. They would therefore engage in drumming and chanting words at the top of their voices to overpower the voices of the crying babies that are cast into the fire during these devilish rituals.

So, in effect the blood of Jesus does not stop the blood of Abel from speaking, but what it does is that it overpowers it, and overwhelms it to the extent that it renders the blood of Abel without effect because if the blood of Jesus is speaking, the voice of the blood of Abel cannot be heard although it's also speaking. Therefore, when one invokes the blood of Jesus into a situation, it introduces into the situation a higher volume, a higher power, and a more perfect vocabulary of expression since it speaks better things.

At times when the people of the world visits the shrine of the fetish priest, they require of them the blood of higher animals due to the gravity of the problem with which they had visited the shrine. At times they are asked to bring the blood of chicken and on other occasions, they are told the blood of chicken will not do. On some occasions the blood of goat is demanded for the rituals. At other times they may be told the blood of human is required for a particular sacrifice for a stronger voice to be heard through the blood that is offered for the sacrifice or ritual. It's because of the varying degree of volume and vocabulary that this higher blood can conjure things in the realm of the spirit.

Notice therefore that if there are any components in the bodies of earthly creatures including humans that is spiritual, none of these components are as spiritual as blood. This is because unlike other components of the body, blood has a mouth, and it also has a voice hence it can speak. However, not only does blood speaks but its' voice can penetrate the realm of the spirit and be heard. That explains why blood is used as the medium to conduct business in the spirit realm. When Abel's blood was shed by his brother, his blood spoke but nobody on earth was able to hear the voice of Abel's blood accept God. This is because the language of blood cannot be understood in the realms of the physical.

What one gains by introducing the blood of Jesus into their situations is that His blood speaks better things than any other blood encoded in the spirit realm against that the person.

3. **Better in Vocabulary**

In the same manner, when Christ died on the cross of Calvary, no one was able to audibly hear the voice of the cry of His blood although there were many people gathered around the cross except for the fact that His voice was heard in the realm of the spirit. As an example, the power of witchcraft and other demonic practices are transacted on some form of blood, so it means there is a vocabulary that is invoked to communicate to spirits in the spirit realm. The spirits then watches over those utterances made through blood, to perform it over the life of the person who is being targeted. However, when one introduces the blood of Jesus into such situation, what one gains by introducing the blood of Jesus is that His blood begins to speak better things than what was encoded in the spirit realm against that person using other blood with lesser power.

The vocabulary used to encode things in the realm of the spirit is dependent on the quality of the blood used. Blood of higher purity and quality has powerful vocabulary and speaks better things than blood of lower quality and purity.

It's worth noting that the vocabulary used to encode things in the realm of the spirit is dependent on the quality of the blood used. Hence to get a higher and more perfect vocabulary, as well as more ability to negotiate in the realm of the spirit, one ought to look for a blood that carries higher or better potency than that which was used against them through witchcraft, so that the capacity to capture a higher intent and power can be achieved. Once that is done through the blood of Jesus, it doesn't matter whatever blood is speaking against that person. Once the blood of Jesus is invoked into the situation on that person's behalf, it has the capacity to utter words which are perfect in both volume, quality, and vocabulary, to overpower whatever blood is speaking against that person in the realm of the spirit.

Blood of Sprinkling; In Old Testament Context

Exodus 24.

> ***24 And he said unto Moses, Come up unto the Lord, thou, and Aaron, Nadab, and***

Abihu, and seventy of the elders of Israel; and worship ye afar off.

2 And Moses alone shall come near the Lord: but they shall not come nigh; neither shall the people go up with him.

3 And Moses came and told the people all the words of the Lord, and all the judgments: and all the people answered with one voice, and said, All the words which the Lord hath said will we do.

4 And Moses wrote all the words of the Lord, and rose early in the morning, and builded an altar under the hill, and twelve pillars, according to the twelve tribes of Israel.

5 And he sent young men of the children of Israel, which offered burnt offerings, and sacrificed peace offerings of oxen unto the Lord.

6 And Moses took half of the blood and put it in basons; and half of the blood he sprinkled on the altar. (The blood of sprinkling)

7 And he took the book of the covenant and read in the audience of the people: and they said, all that the Lord hath said will we do, and be obedient.

8 And Moses took the blood, and sprinkled it on the people, and said, Behold the blood of the covenant, which the Lord hath made with you concerning all these words.

9 Then went up Moses, and Aaron, Nadab, and Abihu, and seventy of the elders of Israel:

10 And they saw the God of Israel: and there was under his feet as it were a paved work of a sapphire stone, and as it were the body of heaven in his clearness.

11 And upon the nobles of the children of Israel he laid not his hand: also, they saw God, and did eat and drink.

12 And the Lord said unto Moses, Come up to me into the mount, and be there: and I will give thee tables of stone, and a law, and commandments which I have written; that thou mayest teach them.

13 And Moses rose up, and his minister Joshua: and Moses went up into the mount of God.

14 And he said unto the elders, Tarry ye here for us, until we come again unto you: and, behold, Aaron and Hur are with you: if any man have any matters to do, let him come unto them.

> ***15 And Moses went up into the mount, and a cloud covered the mount.***
>
> ***16 And the glory of the Lord abode upon mount Sinai, and the cloud covered it six days: and the seventh day he called unto Moses out of the midst of the cloud.***
>
> ***17 And the sight of the glory of the Lord was like devouring fire on the top of the mount in the eyes of the children of Israel.***
>
> ***18 And Moses went into the midst of the cloud, and gat him up into the mount: and Moses was in the mount forty days and forty nights.***

Notice that in the text above God summoned Moses together with a few others to appear before Him, but he ordered for Moses to come closer than the others. What this teaches us is that in the presence of God, we are not the same. Some may dismiss this statement by arguing that.

God is no respecter of persons. Notice however that although God is not a respecter of persons, yet God has respect for those who are intimate with Him. Hence although God doesn't have favorites, but He has intimates. Note that forging an intimate relationship with God is not a gift but rather a deliberate effort on the part of the seeker.

Although God is no respecter of persons,
Yet God respects those who are intimate with Him.

That's why it is no secret that the bible says in Hebrews 11:6 that God is a rewarder of them that diligently seek Him. Diligence has never been named as one of the spiritual gifts in the bible. One's diligence in seeking God comes out of a determined heart and conscious effort on the part of the seeker. It is only people who have a hunger for God can seek Him with diligence. Intimacy is what grants one a special place in the heart of God. The blessedness of intimacy dwells in the fact that when God realized that you have made everything secondary and your seeking Him has become your primary goal, He will carve a special place in His heart for you and treat you different not because He has respect for those He has intimacy with. It is worth noting that God called Abraham His friend based on the intimacy Abraham had with God, to the extent that God said He will not do anything without revealing it to His friend Abraham. God also referred to King David as "a man after God's own heart" because of the intimacy King David had with God. God declared that "*Jacob have I loved, and Esau have I hated*", and one would think that this statement is favoritism on the part of God. However, if you investigate closely the lives of the two brothers Jacob and Esau, you would find out that while Jacob had a heart toward God and toward obeying His will and ordinances, Esau on the other hand was careless in many instances. Esau's carelessness toward God includes his deliberate decision to take wives from the daughters of the heathen nations although it was against the will of his father. Although he was warned against it because such an act was not in alignment with the ordinances of God and the covenants God made with Israel yet, he pursued it.

Thank God for His grace in that although He did not call the others who were with Moses as close to Himself as He did to Moses but at least God give them the privilege to stand afar off so they could see the marvel and the shekinah glory of God when God began to interface with Moses. Moses therefore had the privilege in approaching God closer based on his intimacy with God, to gather instructions upon which the children of Israel will live for generations to come.

The focus in Exodus 24 is in the sixth verse where the sprinkling of the blood is mentioned. The blood was retained in a basin but notice that the first object the blood was sprinkled upon is the altar. After that, Moses took the book of the covenant that contains all the things that Israel was supposed to do to keep in alignment with God. These include the law, the ordinances, the sacrifices and more, and he read it out loud in their hearing. A ceremony had to take place to activate these ordinances which are collectively referred to in this text as the book of the covenant {vs.7} hence that is how the Old Testament became activated. This implies what Moses came down from the mountain with was just a document without the ceremony being performed to activate it. It was just a document because it lacked the signature that would make it a legal and binding covenant between God and man. Therefore, having read it out loud to the congregation and after they have responded that they will do according as is written in the book of the covenant, what then was missing at that point was a signature that will make the book of the covenant legal and binding document that henceforth will be known as the book of the covenant. So, the ceremony was performed and according to the verse 6, and notice that the sprinkling of the blood is what was used as the official signature to make the document a legal binding agreement between man and God.

When the bible speak of the "blood of sprinkling" it is tantamount to having a signature appended on documents to make them legal and binding documents. Without signatures on legal documents, the validity of such documents becomes questionable.

Some people wanting to make a doctrine out of Hebrew 9, which states, *"a testament is not in effect until the Testator dies"* have erroneously held that all that happened in the Old Testament are of no relevance because Christ had not yet gone to the cross at the time hence the death of the Testator had not yet taken place to activate the Testament. In effect what they are saying is that the New Testament really began from the Acts of the Apostles because the timeline for the events recorded in the Acts of the Apostles are after the death of Christ who is the Testator. But if the blood of Jesus, which is the blood of sprinkling represents the signature needed to activate what is written in the body of the document, then that will imply the body of the legal document or covenant was written after the signature which is the blood of Christ was shed. That's not how legal documents or covenants are formulated. A signature (which is represented here by the blood of Jesus) is not signed on documents before the body of the actual document which constitutes the agreement (in this case, the Acts of the Apostles) is formulated. The reverse rather holds true. Documents of agreements are formulated before signatures are appended on them.

Jesus said, ***"I am the resurrection and the life he that believe that in me, although Ye were dead, yet shall he live."***

That's why when you are a true believer, natural death doesn't connect you with the spirit of death. Natural death is a transition into higher realms of life in the spirit. Death could never have authority over Jesus and so it cannot have authority over the believer because of the blood covenant between Christ and the believer in Jesus Christ. In fact, death in the book of revelation is portrayed as a messenger of God. Death served the purposes of God in the book of revelation. Also notice that death when it was created by God, did not have a sting nor power to kill. It was only given a sting over Adam and Eve and over their seed because of the introduction of sin in the garden of Eden through the disobedience of Adam and Eve.

In **Genesis 2:17**, God said to Adam,

> ***17 But of the tree of the knowledge of good and evil, thou shalt not eat of it: for in the day that thou eatest thereof thou shalt surely die.***

The implication here is that if Adam did not eat of the tree of knowledge of good and evil, spiritual death would have had any power over him nor over his seed at all. However, because he disobeyed God and ate the fruit that he was forbidden to eat, the power or the sting of death was activated against Adam and his seed thereafter. Therefore, if anyone threatens you with death, just stare them in the face and tell them that you have no covenant with death as one redeemed by the precious blood of the Lamb of God.

The Blood of Sprinkling in New Testament Context

In the courts of heaven, bible makes us understand that there is this blood of sprinkling that has the right vocabulary.

In this court of heaven, blood can serve as a witness, hence when Abel was killed, it was his blood that served as a witness in the court of heaven against his brother Cain in that the bible says the blood of Abel cried from the ground and based on the testimony of that blood, punishment was imposed upon Cain. As a result, Cain became a vagabond upon the surface of the earth. However, that was just the power and the potency of the blood of Abel who was only an Innocent man. When the blood of Jesus spoke from the ground the moment it touched the ground it was an entirely different blood because it was not the blood of a man who is innocent but rather, of one who had righteous stood with God. So, the blood of Jesus was a righteous blood. The bible calls it the blood of sprinkling that speaketh better things than the blood Abel.

Hebrews 12:24

> ***Unto Jesus the mediator of the new covenant unto the blood of sprinting, that speaker better things than the blood of Abel.***

Notice the above verse says we are come unto the blood of sprinkling. The blood of Abel cried from the ground, so it had a mouth, a voice and it also had vocabulary to express itself before the court of heaven. The voice of that blood rose unto the universal court of heaven, and guess what, its voice was heard that's why God had to intervene by responding to the evil act of murder perpetuated by Cain against his brother Abel. We therefore have two types of blood mentioned here according to this text. The blood of Abel and the blood of Jesus. However, when we come to Zion, we don't come to interact with the blood of Abel, but rather our interface is with the blood of sprinkling which is the blood of Jesus.

In the days of temple worship, once per year the priest sprinkles the blood of bulls and goats that he is offering for the atonement of the sins of the people upon the mercy seat. We know however that it was only a shadow of what was to ultimately come, which is the sprinkling or offering of the blood of Jesus Christ the lamb of God. The blood of Abel was the blood of an innocent man hence it had the ability to cry at the universal court of heaven. The bible says the blood of Abel cried from the ground. It means its voice was projected unto the universal court of heaven by the ground or the earth. Therefore, this then tells us the ground, or the earth may have some potentials that we may not know it all and it is something that is worth looking into. The ground keeps record of what happened on it, and it was the same ground that projected the voice of Abel's blood unto the universal court of heaven.

So, when the first drops of the blood of Jesus touched the ground, the ground took notice and record of it and like the blood of Abel, the ground projected the voice of that blood to the universal court of heaven.

The difference between the blood of Abel and that of Jesus is that while Abel's blood an innocent blood because he was innocently murdered, the blood of Jesus is a righteous blood because Jesus is a righteous man in whom dwells no sin.

Now there is a difference between being an innocent man and being a righteous man and hence between an innocent blood and a righteous blood. One is deemed innocent based on or in reference to a particular circumstance, but it doesn't imply such a person is right or innocent under all circumstances. The righteous on the other hand will always be right because his standing of righteousness is drawn directly from God. Righteousness is a divine standing with reference to God.

As an example, when an innocent blood is shed the repercussions of the shedding of that blood can lead to the death of many others who are innocent, but just because they belong to the bloodline of the person who shed that blood, they suffer consequences. But when you consider the righteous blood of Christ, it's different. When it touched the ground, that was the first time ever that a righteous blood has ever touch the ground, so the ground was amazed, shocked, and so confused that it didn't know what to do with such a blood nor how to handle it and that's why the earth had to quake at the very moment the blood of Jesus touched to ground. In other words, the ground was struggling with what to do with this special and unique kind of blood that it had never handle before. Remember in the history of humanity, countless number of innocent bloods had been shed before, so the ground is familiar with that kind of blood, but what it was new to, was the blood of the righteous son of God.

Before the death of Christ on the cross, the earth had handled many innocent bloods that were shed prior to Calvary, but what the earth had never handled was a righteous blood hence the earth quaked in reaction to the first drops of the blood of Jesus that dropped on it.

Before Christ, the ground had never handled is the blood of a righteous man in the person of Jesus who is sinless and without spot nor wrinkle. It is worth noting that it is that earthquake that run through the foundations of the city and it is that earthquake that was responsible for rending into twain from top to bottom the veil that covered the holy of hollies in the temple. The bible says in Zion, we have come unto that blood, the blood of sprinkling. What this means is that every time you lean on the blood of Jesus, you have passage because the blood can create passages in the spirit that one could never know existed. The children of Israel did not know that a passage under the Red Sea was possible but when the right scepter was lifted [that's the scepter or the rod of Moses] God revealed a passage that led to their great deliverance.

The bible says it is the blood of Jesus that cleanses us from all sins which is the principal work of Satan. The devil's goal for causing humankind to sin is spiritual death and separation from God. Therefore, when we interfere with blood, we are interfering with life or with the path of life and life eternal. Hence by the blood of sprinkling, we have access to God, and we can also access the throne of grace and obtain mercy from God. We are dealing with fact when we deal with the blood, therefore one doesn't have to feel anything to be covered under the blood. In other words, the believer's covering is not based on how one's feeling. You must believe the redemptive and finished work of Christ on the cross because whether you feel something or not, it is factual that the case was settled already before you came into the picture.

Revelation 12:10-11

> ***10 And I heard a loud voice saying in heaven, Now is come salvation, and strength, and the kingdom of our God, and the power of his Christ: for the accuser of our brethren is***

cast down, which accused them before our God day and night.

11 And they overcame him by the blood of the Lamb, and by the word of their testimony; and they loved not their lives unto the death.

"The accuser of the brethren" accuses us day and night. Even when you are asleep Satan doesn't take a break from railing accusations against you. However, the verse 11 says they overcame him by the blood of the lamb and by the word of their testimony. Therefore, matter how many times Satan shows up in the universal court of heaven with a railing accusation against you, the blood of the lamb and the word of your testimony has overcome him. Their testimony became potent because of the blood. That voice and potency of the blood of Jesus caused the earth to quake because the earth couldn't handle it. So, the blood of Jesus speaks forgiveness, deliverance, redemption, mercy, favor and more, therefore there is no doubt it speaks better things than the blood of Abel.

Luke 22:20 declares that at the Lord's supper, Jesus took the cup, saying.

This cup is the new covenant in my blood, which is poured out for you.

Notice that Jesus made it very clear that the new covenant is "in His blood". What Jesus meant by this statement is that His blood will be the signature that will be appended to the new covenant to activate it. This also means that without His blood the New Testament cannot be activated. Hence the validity of the New Testament is based on the blood of

Jesus which is His signature. That's why His blood is referred to in the book of Hebrews as the blood of sprinkling, which is in alignment with the blood that Moses sprinkled Exodus 24 of the Old Testament.

Also notice that after Jesus rose from the dead according to John 20:18, one of the first people Jesus spoke to was Mary Magdalene and the things Jesus spoke to her are recorded in John 20:17. Jesus said to Mary Magdalene

> ***Jesus saith unto her, Touch me not; for I am not yet ascended to my Father: but go to my brethren, and say unto them, I ascend unto my Father, and your Father; and to my God, and your God.***

If Mary was to touch Jesus, that would mean she would have been the only recipient and beneficiary of the redemptive work of Christ on the cross hence the only who would be saved by Jesus' sacrifice of Calvary. That would mean all the sacrifice and salvation Jesus had come to procure for humanity and for generations to come would have all been in vain because it would have benefitted only one person, hence Jesus cautioned Mary not to touch Him but to wait until he had ascended unto the Heavenly Father. The question here is that, how many times will Jesus ascend because before this event, Jesus had ascended a many times already. Jesus made this statement to Mary not because this was His first flight or ascension to heaven but rather because this was the first time He had to ascend with His own blood to offer sacrifice in the throne room of God. All the other times he ascended, it was without blood but on this occasion, it was with His own blood.

Jesus' message to Mary Magdalene was ***"go to tell my brethren that I ascend unto my father and your father, and to my God and your God."***

Later the same day Jesus appeared unto them while the doors were shut for fear of the Jews and said, *"my peace be unto you"* and then Jesus said unto them again after showing them the evidence that He was alive; *"my peace be unto you"*. The first of this saying *"my peace be unto you"*, was to calm their fear because they were shut in for fear of the Jewish and the Roman authorities who carried out the crucifixion of Jesus. However, the second time Jesus uttered the same words *'peace be unto you"* after He had shown them all evidence of his resurrection and cleared their doubts was in the form of a message from his father in heaven. This is because Jesus had offered the peace offering with His own blood in heaven to secure the peace between God and humankind. The peace that was lost in the garden of Eden through Adam and Eve's disobedience.

Resurrection; The legal framework responsible for the judicial basis of our salvation.

In Genesis 2:17 God clearly told Adam that, [17] ***But of the tree of the knowledge of good and evil, thou shalt not eat of it: for in the day that thou eatest thereof thou shalt surely die.***

Since Adam and Eve disobeyed and ate the forbidden fruit, sin became mankind's reward and hence Jesus had to come as the second Adam and through the principle of substitution take man's place in order for mankind to be redeemed and saved from eternal damnation. Since the punishment for Adam and Eve involves death, it implies the only way for Jesus to play the role of a substitute is to die.

Notice however that Jesus was not guilty of the offense He was accused of. Mankind was the ones guilty so He gave himself up by taking our place and became our exchange by the principle of substitution.

As part of the judicial process of His time, Jesus was brought before the Jewish Sanhedrin but notice however that He was not condemn to death by the Torah because He was innocent according to the Torah. All the 613 laws of the Torah couldn't condemn Jesus yet they pushed for His death. Notice also that they brought Him before Pilate, but he could not condemn Jesus either by the Roman law because Pilate, who was a highly trained expect and administrator of the Roman law could not find any fault in Jesus. As a result, the Jewish spiritual authorities devised a doctrine called the 'doctrine of necessity' stating that it was better for one man to die than the whole nation.

John 11:50

> ***"Nor consider that it is expedient for us, that one man should die for the people, and that the whole nation perish not."***

It was based upon the strength of this doctrine they invoked that Jesus was sentenced to death by the Sanhedrin and crucified. Although Jesus was faultless yet they condemn Him to death any way. So when Jesus died, He went to the belly of the earth. A place called Hades where the spirits of death men abode in waiting. The court of heaven had to sit on the case of Jesus and in examining the circumstances under which Jesus was put to death, the judicial system of heaven ruled that the basis upon which Jesus was put to death is false and that He was innocent of all charges brought up against Him. Since it was determined that Jesus was falsely accused, the ruling of the court of Heaven was that He had to be brought back to life. Therefore, the ruling of the court of heaven and the justice that was served by Heaven's judicial system is what became known as the resurrection. Hence through the resurrection of Jesus, He was vindicated, but He had however, already paid the price for the redemption of man through His death.

The price paid therefore became accumulated as currency in the realm of the spirit so that if one believes in Jesus by faith, the currency that has been accumulated in the realm of the spirit is imputed upon him or her as righteousness.

It is worth noting that the Greek word for 'input' means '*it is now logically calculated as righteousness*'. As a result, the sinner who through faith believe in Jesus Christ can now enjoy the full value of the currency as eternal salvation that is able to save the soul of mankind from the curses and wages of sin. So Jesus rose from the death as a sign that He was not allowed in hell. Neither was He allowed in the under-world and in Hades, the place of abode of departed spirits because of the ruling of the court of heaven. When Jesus rose from the death notice that for Him to be justified as being innocent, His blood had to be placed on a balance in Heaven's court of justice and weighed on a scale against the sins of mankind. When this was done, His blood was found to be weightier than the sins of mankind that's why his sacrifice and atonement is able to stand through ages past and ages to come and has the power to blot out the sins of mankind.

When Jesus got to heaven he was given three rewards. The administrative role over the Kingdom of God, which made him God Administrator of the new covenant in his blood. Jesus was also given a ministry whereby he makes intercession for all those who accepts His salvation plan through faith in Christ Jesus. Finally, Jesus was given an office and that office is called the Office of the Christ. (Psalm 110;1-3)

Peter explained further in Acts 2:36 that the day Jesu was sworn into the position as Lord and the Christ in heaven also served as His coronation day and it coincided with the day of Pentecost.

Acts 2:36

> ***"Therefore let all the house of Israel know assuredly, that God hath made the same Jesus, whom ye have crucified, both Lord and Christ".***

Notice that 'Christ' is a title and not a name hence it was officially conferred upon Jesus to now sit upon His throne in heaven and that's when the bible declared in Ephesians 4 that He gave gifts unto men. Notice that Jesus could not give gifts unto men while He was alive on earth. Neither could He do it when He was on the cross or even after He rose from the dead and lived among them for 40 days. Jesus was only able to give out gifts to men after he had ascended up on high according to Ephesians 4:8.

> Ephesians 4*;* [8] ***Wherefore he saith, when he ascended up on high, he led captivity captive, and gave gifts unto men.***
>
> [9] *(Now that he ascended, what is it but that he also descended first into the lower parts of the*

earth? [10] He that descended is the same also that ascended up far above all heavens, that he might fill all things.) [11] And he gave some, apostles; and some, prophets; and some, evangelists; and some, pastors and teachers; [12] For the perfecting of the saints, for the work of the ministry, for the edifying of the body of Christ:

The reason why Jesus couldn't give out gifts unto men any other time was because the coronation had not yet taken place and He did not officially have the title of Lord and The Christ. Notice also that according to the verse 10, Jesus ascended 'far above all heavens', meaning His throne is situated in the highest heaven that could ever be and from there, He fills all things the bible declares. This also refers to a position that depicts His image as being far above all things so He might rightfully rule over all things. Therefore, on one occasion when they referred to Him as 'good' His sharp response is found in Mark 10:18-21 because Jesus did not want to take upon Himself, any glory that has not yet been bestowed upon Him by His Heavenly Father.

Mark 10:18-21 KJV

And Jesus said unto him, why callest thou me good? there is none good but one, that is, God.

Scope of the Potency of the Blood of Jesus

1) It is the blood of sprinkling that gives God the legal rights to forgive sin.

When the accusers of the woman who was caught in the act of adultery brought her to Jesus, her accusers said to Jesus, this woman was caught red-handed in adultery and the law of Moses says she ought to be stoned to death but what say ye about this. Jesus turned to her accusers and said, he among you who have no sin let him cast the first stone, and each of them drop their stones and walk away. What Jesus was trying to say here was that they did not have the authority to enforce those laws of Moses seeing they themselves had lived in guilt of these same laws of Moses. Besides, it takes two to commit the act of adultery, yet they took hold of only the woman caught in adultery and brought her to Jesus while they let go the man who was her partner in the act of adultery.

In that story, Jesus was the only person who had the legality to administer the position of the law and yet He turned to the woman caught in adultery and said to her. *"Neither do I condemned thee, go and sin no more".* What Jesus was saying to this woman is that your accusers cannot condemn you and neither do I condemn thee. But there seem to be a problem with that because justice cannot be equated with pity.

Although Jesus did have forgiveness but under the law of Moses there was no such thing as "forgiveness" because the law doesn't recognized forgiveness.

Sins were not forgiven under the law of Moses but rather, they were covered. Meaning those sins were still there but so God would not have to look upon it, God allowed it to be covered with blood. Hence the only grounds upon which Jesus had to let the woman go was that in a few days' time, Jesus was going to go on the cross to establish the covenant that guaranteed forgiveness of sin. That can be likened to using a credit card which works on the principle of "buy now and pay later". Therefore, Jesus bought her pardon or forgiveness of sin, only so He could pay for it in a matter of few days away on the cross of Calvary.

Hebrews 10:22 admonishes the believer as follows,

> ***"Let us draw near with true heart in full assurance of faith, having our hearts sprinkled from evil conscience, and our bodies washed with pure water".***

Hence, the blood of Jesus has the potency to sprinkle our heart from evil conscious.

2) The blood is a token of God's redemptive work.

The word "token" means a receipt which serves as proof of payment. So, when you present the blood of Jesus, what you are presenting before Satan is the receipt, which is the proof of your redemption and the fact that your sins have fully been paid for by the redemptive work of Christ. Remember that since the devil is "the accuser of the brethren" as the bible portray him to be, it means the devil will always bring up the issue of ownership. Satan will come and bombard your mind with different thoughts, challenges, and accusations. This Satan does to try to convince you that he still owns your life. That's why you need a token or a receipt of payment, so that when Satan comes, you can show him the proof that you have been redeemed and purchased and that Christ has fully paid the price for that purchase through His blood that was shed on Calvary for you. The token is a very strong grounds for argument against Satan for your liberty in Christ. Therefore, every time Satan stands before you with accusations, or condemnation of your past and tells you that based on divine legal grounds you have sinned no use to pray, you just need to remind Satan of the words of a popular hymn written by G.T. Haywood entitled "I see a crimson stream of blood".

1) On Calvary's hill of sorrow.
Where sin's demands were paid,
And rays of hope for tomorrow.
Across our path were laid

2) When gloom and sadness whisper,
"You've sinned, no use to pray,"
I look away to Jesus,
And He tells me to say:

Refrain
I see a crimson stream of blood,
It flows from Calvary,
Its waves which reach the throne of God,
Are sweeping over my soul.

APPENDIX 1

AUDIO TAPES BY THE AUTHOR

There are 3 phases to freedom. Bondage, Deliverance and Change in Mindset. Deliverance is not the same thing as Freedom because while deliverance is instantaneous, freedom is a process. Strikingly and interestingly, the Nation of Israel, Our Lord Jesus Christ, as well as every New Testament Believer, started their journey of faith from Egypt (Bondage).

- We all must go through our first body of water (Red Sea)
- We all must go through our share of trials & temptations (Wilderness)
- We all must cross our second body of water (Jordan)
- But not all will be able to get to the promise land of Canaan (Freedom)

The 4 Degrees of Relationship, Friends; Choose godly, choose wisely. (Part 1-7)

We all have some form of associations within our sphere of life. Our success or failure in life hangs strongly on the nature of our associations. In this 7 part teaching series Dr. Nyarko expounds on the key ingredients to a wise, healthy and godly relationship using the example of Jesus as our model. Dr. Nyarko's approach to this subject will leave you amused, instructed, enlightened, stirred up, and challenged but definitely not bored.

Understanding Kingdom Authority (Part 1-3)

Many folks in church know that there is power in the blood of Jesus only a few knows how this power goes to work for humanity. In this 3-part series audio tape, you will be blown away by the in-depth teachings by Dr. Nyarko on the Blood of Jesus and why he is referred to as the Lamb of God.

WHILE MEN SLEPT. (Part 1 & 2)

This message depicts "A wild Bull caught in a net."
(Isaiah 52:20) which in a way, is the Portrait of a Sleeping Church which although has been endowed with great power yet ensnared by little things.

THE STATE OF SIN & THE ACT OF SIN

There is a striking difference between the state of sin and the act of sin. Here is a brief definition of the two. "All have sinned and come short the glory of God". That is the state of sin. But after salvation, the bible also says, "if we confess our sins, he is faithful and just to forgive and cleanse us from all unrighteousness". That is the act of Sin. How are they handled?

THE MANTLE & THE SPIRIT.

Elisha received a double portion of Elijah's anointing but what does this really mean? He received a mantle, and he also received a spirit transfer.

PRAYER: THE POWER OF PETITIONING
(Parts 1-4)

The is the most exercised event of the church and yet the least understood act in the church. Prayer, for many has been turned into presenting a 'shopping list' to God. This series of messages on prayer deals with the legal grounds of what it means to present a petition to God.

This is a timely message of accountability for every Believer. God's prime purpose for creating man, according to the book of Genesis was to find a Manager for all His creation. Hence God will first test our trustworthiness before He entrust anything into our care. This is because to him the much is given, much shall be required, the bible says.

THE ACT OF WORSHIP

This 3 series tape will leave you amused and enlightened but not bored. It is an in-depth exposition of Psalm 149 and reveals how true worship should be in the sanctuary of our God based on the meaning of the common word Hallelujah. (Halal Yah)

The story of Job is one that is hard to comprehend with. It has more 'why' than answers. It always leads to the age-old question of "Why should the Righteous Suffer"? This series of tapes will bring answers as well as comfort to you in your moments of suffering. Listen to it and pass the message on.

Have you ever thought of the fact that God does not live in time but created time for man to live in.? Time is the most precious commodity that we have as humans. While we may have different ethnic backgrounds, may differ in knowledge, wealth, education etc., we are all given the same amount of time within each day. Therefore, what you end up becoming, is largely dependent on how you use your time. Time is too precious to waste so make sure you don't let it slip out of your hands unawares.

We are saved momentarily when we surrender our lives to Christ and accept His Lordship over our lives, however

growing into perfection is not attained overnight. It is a gradual and progressive work of God that can only take place with the cooperation of an individual with the work of the Holy Spirit.

THE 7TH RESURRECTION.

This is an Easter message of hope both in the present and future for the child of God who looks to the saving power of the cross in his or her daily life. While it is true that Christ died and resurrected for the sake of sinful humanity, it is worth noting also that His death and especially his resurrection was the 7th resurrection account in the entire bible. It was the 7th because the number seven is a symbol of perfection, and His resurrection was meant to perfect all that had occurred before Him in that it was the only resurrection

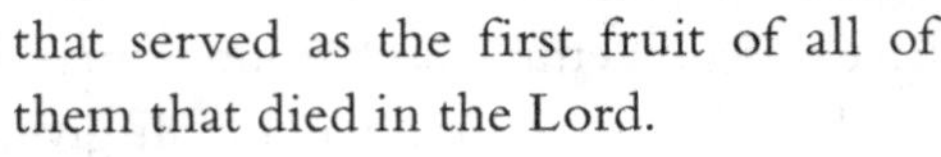

that served as the first fruit of all of them that died in the Lord.

This book is about the biblical story of Cain and Abel, the first products of human procreation through Adam and Eve. This story is unique in that there are a couple of things done that were unknowns to human history. It is a story that although began with God's judgement against sinful human nature inherited through Adam and Eve, however, it ends with the powerful act of redemption that only comes from a God of second chances.

God said, *"I will pour out My Spirit in the last days upon all flesh"*. This began at Pentecost only as minor beginning. Before Christ's return, the Holy Spirit will precede in immanence, power, and glory, to prepare the church, because Christ isn't coming for a defeated church still struggling with sin and divisions, but a glorious church without spot nor wrinkle. The dimension of outpouring of God's Spirit will depend on how desirous the church is for His presence. After the earth opens its mouth due to dryness and desire rain from God, former and latter rains of revival are the fulfillment of this desire. Isaiah 37:3b *says "for the children are come to birth and there is not strength to deliver"* May it never be said of today's church that we came close to birth and had no strength to deliver. *Read, Repent, Be Revived.*

Printed in the United States
by Baker & Taylor Publisher Services